Contents

Preface

Introduction   1

1 Monolingual classes   4
- a quiz   4
- multilingual and monolingual classes   5
- native and non-native speaker teachers   6
- advantages of non-native speaker teachers in monolingual classes   7
- questions and further activities   11
- references   11

2 The L1 in the classroom: some general points   12
- a health warning   12
- the other side of the story   13
- the right balance   14
- a questionnaire   15
- L1 problem clinics   18
- questions and further activities   19
- references   19

3 The role of the L1 in presenting and practising new language   20
- the importance of presentation and practice   20
- grammatical form, meaning and the L1   20
- some common presentation and practice techniques   22
- the role of the L1   25
- getting meaning across   37
- questions and further activities   39
- references   39

4 Pair and group work in monolingual classes   40
- the importance of pair and group work   40
- organising a class for pair and group work   41
- making pair and group activities work   42
- the role of the L1   47
- dealing with too much L1 use   49
- conclusion   51
- questions and further activities   51
- references   52

5 Using translation activities — 53
- some benefits of using translation activities — 53
- some criticisms of translation — 54
- what is a good translation? — 55
- translation and fluency activities — 57
- true cognates and false friends — 59
- some translation activities for the classroom — 61
- questions and further activities — 65
- reference — 65

6 Making progress in the classroom — 66
- learner training — 66
- setting and achieving realistic aims — 74
- motivation and class control — 76
- dealing with discipline problems — 80
- questions and further activities — 82
- references — 83

7 Making progress outside the classroom — 84
- homework — 85
- reading — 87
- listening and watching — 88
- self-access centres — 89
- speaking and writing — 90
- questions and further activities — 91
- useful addresses — 91
- references — 91

8 'English only' and bilingual dictionaries — 92
- 'English only' learner's dictionaries — 92
- bilingual dictionaries — 95
- questions and further activities — 97
- references — 97

9 Basic classroom English — 98
- using the tables — 103
- questions and further activities — 104

Appendix: 10 tips for teachers who don't know their students' language — 105

Preface

MOST LEARNERS OF English can be found in 'monolingual' classes – classes where all the students share a common language other than English. Yet, much of the literature on language teaching nowadays tends to concentrate on the 'multilingual' situation, i.e. where students come from a variety of different backgrounds and can only communicate with each other and the teacher through English.

This gap in the literature is unfortunate, because monolingual classes have their own special characteristics, and approaches which work well in a multilingual situation are not necessarily appropriate for teachers of monolingual groups. For example, there is the question of the students' first language and the role it can play – *does* play, sometimes whether we like it or not! – within the classroom.

A very common approach nowadays is to try to ban the first language ('L1') from the classroom completely, and to use only the 'direct method'. In the direct method, all communication in the classroom is supposed to take place in English, or through gesture and mime. In fact, many teachers feel rather guilty if they allow the students' L1 to be used at all. One of the main purposes of this book is to show how teachers can use a modern, communicative methodology which integrates selective and limited use of the L1, to answer the crucial question which is all too often avoided – *When is it appropriate to use the L1?* David Atkinson indicates not only situations when the L1 can be used, he also suggests that there are times when there are enormous advantages in using it – an acknowledgement that many teachers will welcome. At the same time, he also shows that use of the L1 can be abused, too.

Focusing as it does on the use of the L1 and other issues which are particularly important in monolingual classes, this book will be welcomed by teachers who feel the need for sound, realistic advice on teaching monolingual groups of learners.

Neville Grant

To Nuria and Marc

Acknowledgements

I would like to thank Alyson Lee and Lisa Howard at Longman and Neville Grant, the series editor, for helping to make this a better book than it would have been without their detailed comments and support.

I would also like to thank the following people for all the phone calls and more: Tony Wright, Jill Cadorath, Jenny Bradshaw, Joc Potter, Andy Hopkins and Jeremy Harmer. It goes without saying that all faults and weaknesses are my own responsibility.

Introduction

What is a monolingual class?

A monolingual English class is one where the students all have a common language other than English (and often a common culture too); for example, Japanese in a class in Tokyo, Arabic in a class in Cairo, etc. Most monolingual English classes take place in countries where English is not the main language. However, it's quite possible to imagine, say, a group of Cantonese speakers being taught in the USA or a class of French speakers learning English in London.

This book focuses particularly on monolingual classes where the teacher also knows the students' language. In most cases this is because the teacher is a native speaker of that language; for example a Japanese teacher teaching Japanese students. In addition to this, there are obviously large numbers of native (English) speakers who know their learners' language. This is true, for instance, of many British teachers in European countries, or many teachers from the USA working in Latin America. There are also, of course, a lot of teachers of monolingual classes who *don't* know their students' language. Much of this book will also be relevant for them.

Why a book on monolingual classes?

The great majority of teachers of English in the world teach monolingual classes. The 'multilingual' situation, where a native speaker of English teaches groups of mixed nationalities, is of course common in Britain, the USA, Australia and Canada. But, in most countries, it is relatively unusual. Monolingual classes are *different* from multilingual classes; and in very important ways. For example, the students' 'L1', that is, the language which they share other than English, can be a problem in the classroom. Many

> **How can I use more English in the class?**

teachers feel, quite rightly, that they and their students may be in danger of using it too much. However, the L1 can be a valuable resource if it is used at appropriate times and in appropriate ways. The question is:

> Should English be spoken *all* the time by *all* teachers of English in *all* classes?

> **Is it really necessary to always use English?**

This book answers that question by suggesting ways in which teachers can use the L1 as a resource without allowing it to be over-used. One of the book's main purposes is:

> To help teachers to use as much English as possible without feeling that the L1 should never be used in class.

The contents of this book

The first two chapters deal with the special characteristics of monolingual classes and make some important points about the L1 in the classroom. Then, in chapters three and four, we take two types of classroom activity and look closely at the question of the L1 in them. These are:

- presentation and practice of new language
- pair and group work.

These are areas where the teacher needs to have a clear attitude towards the role of the L1, but it is important to remember that in *any* activity the teacher needs to make decisions about whether or not the L1 should be used. The general guidelines given in these two chapters will help you to do that.

The second part of the book deals with a number of other important aspects of monolingual classes: using translation activities, helping students to learn as much as possible both inside and outside the classroom, and the advantages and disadvantages of various types of dictionaries. The final chapter provides check-lists of the sort of English that all teachers and students should be using routinely in the classroom.

Some terms used in this book

- *Native speaker teachers* are teachers whose first language is English.
- *Non-native speaker teachers* are teachers whose first language is not English, e.g. a Turkish or Italian teacher of English. However, a lot of what is said in this book about non-native speakers will also be true of native speakers who have a good knowledge of their students' language and culture.
- *The L1* is the common language that the students (and sometimes the teacher) share in a monolingual class. This common language isn't necessarily the *mother tongue* of everyone in the classroom. For example, in a class in Madrid the L1 is usually Spanish, but the mother tongue of some of the students might be Catalan or Basque. Similarly, in a Hong Kong class, some of the students using Cantonese as an 'L1' might have Mandarin or Hokkien as their mother tongue.

Questions and further activities

1 Has most of your own language learning experience been in monolingual or multilingual situations? If you have experience of both, which did you prefer and why?
2 Make lists of, in your opinion, the main advantages and disadvantages of *not* knowing your students' language. Which seem more important, the advantages or disadvantages?

Monolingual classes

A quiz

In this chapter, we are going to look at some of the advantages and disadvantages of the following:

- Multilingual and monolingual classes.
- Native and non-native speaker teachers.

The following short 'quiz' will help to put this discussion into a global context.

ACTIVITY

Decide whether you think each of the following statements is true or false. Put a ✓ or a X in each case.

1 More than a quarter of the world's population uses English regularly. ☐

2 More than 500 million people can speak English reasonably well. ☐

3 More than one billion (1,000,000,000) people have some competence in English. ☐

Obviously, it is difficult to give exact figures for questions of this kind. But, the answers which follow are reasonably reliable.

1 Clearly, it depends on what we mean by 'regularly'. But most experts agree that the correct proportion is approximately a quarter or more. ✓

2 Again, 'reasonably well' can mean a lot of things. However, we do know that there are about 300 million native speakers of English. In addition, there are certainly far more than 200 million non-native speakers in the world who speak at least 'reasonable' English. So, the total is definitely more than 500 million. ✓

3 Opinions on this vary (how much English do you need to know to have 'some competence'?). But most estimates are of more than a billion; some are as high as 2 billion! ✓

What do these statistics mean for the English language teacher? Among other things, they show quite clearly that English is a *resource* which is used by enormous numbers of people in the world, and that the majority of these people are not native speakers of English. We can make three very important points about this:

1. English is no longer the 'property' of any one country or culture. There is no longer 'one' English language, but many varieties of it.
2. Many non-native speakers of English use English to communicate with other non-native speakers.
3. Many learners of English have no need to learn about British or American culture (or the culture of any of the other countries where English is the main language).

All of this has significant implications for the roles of native speakers and non-native speakers in teaching English.

Traditionally, native speakers were thought to be the ideal kind of teacher. This was partly because they usually had (or were thought to have) a 'deep' knowledge of British (or North American, or Australian) culture and also because they were a 'perfect model' of English for their learners. Many people now feel that these factors are becoming less important in the modern world.

> English is a world language and fewer learners need to reach a 'native-like' level in it. And anyway, there are a lot of 'non-native speakers' who have a better knowledge of English (and English-speaking cultures) than many native speakers.

Don't multilingual classes have a lot of advantages?

For readers of journals such as *World Englishes*, these points are quite obvious nowadays. Unfortunately, however, many teachers and teacher trainers still seem to assume that native speakers make the best teachers and that 'multilingual' classes are the best kind of class. Is there really any truth in these assumptions? We're now going to examine both of them in more detail, starting with the question of multilingual versus monolingual classes.

Multilingual and monolingual classes

Multilingual classes have a number of advantages. Some of these, with their implications for teachers of monolingual classes, are:

Multilingual classes	Implications for monolingual classes
1 Multilingual classes usually take place in an English-speaking environment. This means that learners often have a lot of opportunities to practise English outside the classroom.	Teachers of monolingual classes need to encourage students to use every chance to study or practise outside class time (see chapter 7). However in many situations, audio and video cassettes can help teachers give students a lot more exposure to native speaker English within the classroom.
2 The learners bring different cultures and diverse backgrounds to the classroom. This can be stimulating and motivating.	Teachers should be aware of as many ways as possible of making classroom activities interesting and enjoyable. (See, for example, chapter 4.)
3 The learners' only common language is English. For this reason, practice in English can be very realistic and enjoyable.	Although this book deals with the question of when L1 use is appropriate, I've included reminders that English *must* be the main classroom language. There's no reason why 'all English' activities shouldn't be very successful in monolingual classes (see chapter 4).

> ACTIVITY
> Make a list of any additional advantages of multilingual classes.

The advantages that multilingual classes have are clearly important. However, the monolingual situation also has powerful advantages of its own. In reality, it's impossible to say that one type of class or teacher is simply 'better' than another – it all depends on so many things. For many learners the ideal would be a *combination* of monolingual and multilingual learning although such an opportunity obviously doesn't exist for most learners.

Native and non-native speaker teachers

It is easy to think of convincing reasons why native speakers of English have a lot of advantages as teachers of the language:

- It is sometimes easier for students to feel confident that a native speaker teacher really knows English well.
- In general (but not always), it's easier for native speakers to be confident that the English they're using is appropriate.
- Native speakers usually have fewer problems of words which they don't know coming up in class. (However, non-native speakers are often better at explaining points of grammar. *All teachers have to deal with questions which they can't answer on the spot; there's nothing wrong with telling a group that you'll look something up and tell them next lesson.*)
- In many cases, it's easier for native speakers to insist on students using English in the classroom, especially if they don't know the students' language.

Again, these are important points. But as with monolingual/multilingual classes, it doesn't make sense to say that native speakers or non-native speakers are simply 'better'. In this case too, the ideal thing for most learners is probably a combination of the two types of teacher.

It is quite clear, then, that multilingual classes and native speaker teachers have many positive features. However, the equally important positive aspects of monolingual classes and non-native speaker teachers tend to be discussed much less frequently.

Advantages of non-native speaker teachers in monolingual classes

We can divide the special resources of non-native speaker teachers in monolingual classes into three main areas:

1. Knowledge of the English language and language learning.
2. Knowledge of the students' L1.
3. Knowledge of the students' environment and culture.

Knowledge of the English language and language learning

The English language

Almost all non-native speakers have studied English at some time. Their knowledge of English may not be as *complete* as a native speaker's, but they have thought about and struggled with the language. Many non-native speakers have a sophisticated knowledge of the structure of English, a kind of knowledge which native speakers can only develop with special training or long years of classroom experience. Non-native speakers tend to have a better idea than many native speakers of how English works.

Language learning

All non-native speaker teachers of English are language learners themselves. They all speak at least two languages and they've all learned English as a foreign language. They've experienced themselves the difficulties which their students have. This puts them in a very good position to understand those difficulties.

While it is true that many native speaker teachers (although by no means all) have also learned other languages successfully, they haven't learned *English* as a foreign language. For this reason it is difficult for them to have the same sort of understanding of students' difficulties as non-native teachers often have.

Knowledge of the students' L1

What to teach and what to concentrate on

Many errors have their causes in the L1. Knowledge of the L1 is therefore a very important tool for the teacher. Teachers who know the learners' L1 are in a much better position to know which aspects of English to concentrate on in their teaching. In a multilingual class almost any aspect of the language will cause difficulties for some of the students. But in a monolingual class teachers have the opportunity to concentrate on more specific problems. From this point of view, teaching in monolingual classes can be extremely efficient.

You've probably also found in your teaching that your students' L1 isn't the cause of all their errors. Learners often make mistakes which you wouldn't expect them to make, and they don't make some mistakes which you would expect them to make. A lot of learners develop a sort of 'language of their own' (an *interlanguage*) as they learn so it isn't only the influence of their L1 and the obvious problems of the way English works which make them sound different from a native speaker. It's very difficult to see exactly what the cause of this kind of error is. It doesn't seem to be traceable back to the L1 or any aspect of English grammar.

The influence of the L1 is the key to many errors, but teachers shouldn't expect it to provide explanations for all the problems which their students have.

> ACTIVITY
> A Make a list of the main pronunciation problems which your learners have. Does the coursebook (or other material) which you work with cover these problems? Do your materials deal with any aspects of pronunciation which *don't* cause problems for your learners?
> B Look again at your coursebook. Does it include any areas of *grammar* which don't cause your learners any difficulties?

Activities in the classroom

The teacher of monolingual classes has the option of making use of the students' L1 in the classroom. As I suggested in the introduction, the L1 can be a very valuable resource if it is used appropriately. This is a topic which we'll concentrate on later in the book.

Knowledge of the students' environment and culture

In most monolingual classes the learners come from similar backgrounds and live in similar environments. Teachers who are familiar with these aspects of the learners' lives are in a better position to help them learn. Such teachers have (or can get) a good idea about, amongst other things, the following important factors:

A the learners' educational backgrounds;

B their expectations about how teachers should teach and learners should learn;

C their knowledge of the world;

D similarities and differences between the learners' culture and English-speaking cultures;

E the learners' knowledge of English-speaking cultures;

F what sort of topics the students might find motivating and the sorts of ways in which the students might need to use English in the future.

A and B: Teachers who are familiar with (or who have actually experienced as students) the educational system of their students' culture have a great advantage. They are likely to know what sort of activities students are familiar with, what they expect the teacher to do in the classroom and what approaches they might find strange or uncomfortable. For instance, some learners find pair and group work 'embarrassing', or 'useless', or 'stupid', often because they are not used to it. Obviously, it is not a question of the teacher always doing things in ways which meet students' expectations, but it is extremely important to be aware of what their expectations *are*. Introducing unfamiliar techniques gradually and 'gently' can be a useful approach (more about this in chapter 4).

C: If a teacher is aware of what the students know about the world, it can be much easier to choose appropriate and interesting activities for the classroom. For example, with a class of adolescents it can be very risky to use songs in the classroom without having a good idea of what their tastes in music are! We'll also look more at this question in chapters 4 and 7.

D and E: We said earlier that a teacher who knows the students' L1 can decide more easily which aspects of the L2 are likely to cause difficulties. The same is true when students need or want to know about an English-speaking culture. The teacher who 'knows' both cultures will know which aspects are similar and which aspects of the English-speaking culture might be unfamiliar or difficult to understand. For example, in Japanese culture the idea of 'politeness' is very different from most English-speaking cultures. Ideally, a teacher of Japanese students will have a good knowledge of how politeness works in *both* cultures.

F: Where the future needs of the learners are clear, teachers can try to relate classroom activities both to these and to their everyday interests.

Finally, we should also mention the fact that in many monolingual situations the teacher is there not only to teach the language, but to *educate* the students; for example, in primary and secondary schools. Many people feel that education is a job which is best done, most of the time, by teachers who are from the same culture as the learners – that is, non-native speakers of English. They believe that one of the main purposes of education is to help young people to develop a secure identity rooted in their own culture, while also developing respect for and interest in other cultures and languages. In this sense, it's interesting to note that some recent research suggests that native speakers using the direct method need to take care in some circumstances not to cause 'cultural disorientation' among their students (see reference 2 below).

In this chapter then, we've emphasised that it's very important for teachers to know as much as possible about their students' language, culture and environment. In multilingual classes this is often very difficult, because there are so many kinds of students in the same class. In monolingual classes, however, one of the teacher's biggest advantages is that generally students have the same background and L1.

Questions and further activities

1 Imagine that you are going to learn a new foreign language in your own country. What are the most important characteristics that your teacher should have? Does it matter whether he or she is a native speaker or not? Why (not)?
2 In this chapter (page 9) you did an activity where you looked at differences in pronunciation and grammar between an L1 and an L2. Now make a list of ways of giving advice (e.g. 'If I were you, I'd . . .') and of apologising (e.g. 'I really am sorry about . . .') in English. How many of these ways can you translate literally into your own language (or another language you know well) without their sounding unnatural? How similar or different are ways of apologising and advising in the two languages?
3 Which aspects (if any) of an English-speaking culture do *your* learners need to know about? Which aspects are particularly difficult for them to understand?
4 Is it really possible to teach a language without teaching about a culture too? If so, is this a good thing?

References

1 The statistics given in the quiz are based on an article by David Crystal in *English Today* Issue 1 January 1985 (Cambridge)
2 *Linguistic Imperialism* by Robert Phillipson (Oxford 1992, page 193)

The L1 in the classroom: some general points

A health warning

Isn't it better to keep the L1 out of the classroom, especially in monolingual classes where students only have a few hours of English per week? Surely, the more L1 is used the less English practice students get? As teachers, we have to face the fact that:

> Every second spent using the L1 is a second *not* spent using English! – And every second counts!

It's so easy to start by using the L1 'now and again', because it's easier or more convenient. But any teacher has to be very careful, because 'now and again' can quickly become a routine where, before you know it, the L1 becomes the *main* language of the classroom. This must be avoided at all costs, because:

> If English is *not* the main language used in the classroom, the learners are not going to learn very much English.

This is for many reasons, including the following:

- Listening to English is *learning* English. The more students listen to English in the classroom, the more they revise what they know and increase their knowledge. They also acquire a lot of language which isn't necessarily the main focus of a particular lesson.
- If you want to learn to play the piano, you have to *play* the piano. We don't know very much about how learning takes place, but we do know that you can't learn a language without practising. The more students practise English in the classroom, the better their English will become.
- It's very difficult to learn English by listening to someone talking *about* English in French, Russian, Arabic or any other language. If English is the normal means of communication in the

classroom, it is easier for learners to see that it's a real language and not 'just another subject'.
- Routine use of English helps learners adapt to 'real' situations outside the classroom. They need to get used to listening to the 'message' of what is said, rather than trying to understand every word. Similarly, they practise communicating a message without worrying about whether it is completely 'correct'.

> Quite simply, too much use of the L1 is probably the single biggest danger in any monolingual class.

The other side of the story

Should we use mainly English in the classroom? is one question where the answer is definitely 'yes'. But . . . *Should we use only English?* is another. (This is sometimes called the 'direct method'.)

As the diagram below suggests, there are all sorts of stages between one hundred-per-cent direct method and a classroom dominated by the L1.

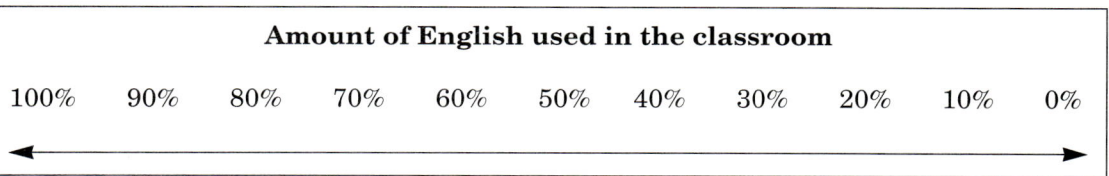

I have talked to many teachers about this question and it seems that many of them often feel slightly guilty about using the L1 in the classroom at all. They feel that they are not achieving the 'ideal' of one hundred-per-cent English. But, should one hundred-per-cent direct method *be* an ideal in all monolingual classes? It's always important to use as much English as possible, but the L1 *can* be a vital resource, and there is certainly no reason why any teacher of monolingual classes should feel that it is somehow 'wrong' to make use of it.

Learning a language is a difficult and often frustrating process for many learners, particularly at low levels. One hundred-per-cent direct method can be especially stressful and frustrating – limited use of the L1 can have a powerful, positive effect here. For many learners (in particular adults and teenagers), occasional use of the L1 gives them the opportunity to show that they are intelligent, sophisticated people.

> ACTIVITY
>
> Where are *you* on the diagram on page 13 as regards the amount of L1 used in your classes? Can you think of ways in which you could increase the amount of English used? For example, in the area of classroom routines, or presentation of new language.

The right balance

But what's the right balance between English and the L1?

We can say quite clearly that there isn't a simple 'right balance'. English (or any other language being taught) should be the language used for the vast majority of the time in *any* class. But the exact proportions of English and L1 will depend on many factors:

- *The students' previous experience.* If you find yourself teaching students who have been used to classes taking place mainly in the L1, you may very well need to increase the amount of English used in a gradual way.
- *Level.* The higher the level, the less reason there is to use the L1. At higher levels it should be unnecessary, for example, for purposes of class management. But it can still be useful in other areas, e.g. translation of vocabulary (see chapter 5).
- *The stage of the course.* In general, one of the main aims of a teacher with a new group should be to decrease gradually the amount of L1 used. As the teacher gets to know the students and the students become familiar with the teacher's style, it becomes easier to do more activities entirely in English.
- *The stage of the lesson.* There are times when the L1 should never be used (see chapter 3 for some examples). On the other hand, there are some activities in which the L1 can play a central role (for instance 'L1 problem clinics' discussed later in this chapter).

It's impossible, therefore, to talk about an 'ideal' proportion of English and L1. What we *can* do, however, is to look at some circumstances in which the L1 might be used and ask whether this would be justified in each case.

A questionnaire

In which of the following circumstances (if any) do you think use of the L1 is justified? Tick 'Yes' (justified) or 'No' (not justified) according to your opinion in each case.

		Yes	No
1	I want that student at the back to open the window. They are only level 1 and she won't understand if I ask her in English.		✓
2	I've tried everything to get them to understand what *vase* means. I'll just have to translate it.	✓?	
3	I've tried everything to get them to understand what *unusual* means. I'll just have to translate it.	✓	
4	They really can't take any more. I'll give them a two minute rest period in which they can speak to each other in the L1.	✓	
5	He obviously feels that what he's trying to say is important, but I really can't understand what he means. I'll get him to say it in the L1, then I'll help him to translate it into English.	?	
6	'My Portuguese is getting much better; my students are really impressed!' (native speaker of English)		✓
7	My students feel silly if I ask them to speak English together.		✓
8	I make lots of mistakes when I use English. I'd better not use it too much or my students will 'learn' the same mistakes.		?
9	My students make a lot of mistakes when they use English. I'd better not ask them to use too much of it.		✓
10	They're too young to do very much in English.		✓
11	Something very interesting has just happened in an English-speaking country. My students really want to discuss it, but their level's too low for them to do this in English.	✓	
12	They really haven't understood the grammar we've been doing recently. Perhaps we should try discussing it in the L1.	✓	

We'll take the situations one by one:

1 *I want the window at the back open. The student won't understand if I ask in English.* Is it really impossible to get them

to understand? Mime and gesture to accompany the English would almost certainly be enough. It's vital that, where possible, 'real' communication takes place in English. Otherwise, students (particularly younger students) can feel that English is just something which happens in exercises or drills.

2 *The students don't understand* vase. *I'll translate it.* Has this teacher tried drawing? Okay, some teachers 'can't draw', but surely anyone could manage something vaguely resembling a vase. Translation is simply unnecessary here. And anyway, sometimes a direct 'image' can be a much more powerful stimulus than a translation.

Note: For teachers who feel they can't draw, see Andrew Wright and Safia Haleem's book in this series *Visuals for the Language Classroom* (Longman 1991).

3 *The students don't understand* unusual. *I'll translate it.* It is possible to 'explain' what this word means by using, say, examples or a definition. But this can be unreliable and time-consuming. *Unusual* is the sort of abstract word where translation can be the simplest, quickest solution. (See chapter 3.)

4 *I'll give the students two minutes to talk in their L1.* Some people would argue that a two minute L1 'rest' period is a wasted two minutes; they may be right. But, if it's two minutes out of a fifty minute lesson, we have to look at the whole lesson. If a two minute L1 break after thirty minutes means that more effective work is done in the last eighteen minutes, then the break might be worth it. Of course, one has to be careful; but a chance to 'let off steam' in the L1 can have its place, particularly with younger learners whose concentration isn't very good.

5 *A student is trying to explain something in English. I can't understand. I'll help him to translate from the L1 into English.* It can be terribly frustrating for learners, especially in 'communicative' activities, if they can't make others understand what they're trying to say. There's no reason why teachers shouldn't allow the learners to express themselves in the L1 and then help them to express the same idea in English. But this technique should be used with caution. Part of learning a language is having to make an effort to communicate – teachers who constantly 'spoonfeed' their students are not helping them.

6 *I'll impress my students with my Portuguese.* The classroom is *not* the place for native speakers to practise your foreign languages. If a native speaker uses the L1 in the classroom, it should be for a good reason connected with the *students'* learning of English.

7 *My students feel silly speaking English together.* Feelings of 'silliness' can be a real problem, particularly with adolescents. But if the teacher doesn't succeed in doing something about it, the students will certainly learn less. (See chapter 4.)

8 *My English is full of mistakes.* No teacher's English is perfect (non-native speaker *or* native speaker!) but less than perfect English is better than no English. Obviously, it's important not to worry about this too much – very frequently, the more you worry about it, the more mistakes you make.

9 *My students make a lot of mistakes in English.* Making mistakes is part of learning a language. If students wait until they're 'perfect' before practising, they'll *never* learn to use the language. Practice and mistakes are absolutely essential.
Note: For more on this, see *Mistakes and Correction* in this series by Julian Edge (Longman 1989).

10 *They're too young to learn very much in English.* This is a complicated question. But we *can* say that for some young children classes entirely in English can be very disorientating and negative. On the other hand, for some children the English class can be an exciting, different world, where everything happens in a different language. There's no easy answer here. The best solution will depend on the kind of group and the teacher. However, it's always worth remembering that many children can develop the ability to understand a lot in a foreign language long before they're able to say very much.

11 *Some very important news has just happened. My students want to discuss it but their English is not good enough.* There's no reason not to have a *brief* L1 discussion – the attention given to the event might be very good for motivation. In addition to this, the teacher might like to prepare a whole lesson (given in the L2!) with the same event as the 'theme'.

12 *The students haven't understood much of the grammar we have studied recently. Should we discuss it in the L1?* This is an important point. The short answer is that discussion of problematic aspects of English in the L1 can be a justifiable and useful activity. This is the topic of the next section on 'L1 problem clinics'.

It is sometimes said that teachers should use 'English where possible' and 'L1 where necessary'. We can perhaps say that the questions which teachers need to ask themselves are:

> Can I justify using the L1 here?
>
> Will it help the students' learning more than using English would?

L1 problem clinics

L1 'problem' sessions can help to sort out all kinds of difficulties. Some teachers make 'L1 problem clinics' a regular feature of their classes, say once a week or once a month. The students know in advance that there's going to be a 'clinic', so they have time to think about areas of difficulty which they want to ask about in the L1.

Making 'clinics' of this kind part of your teaching can be very useful from the point of view of motivation. If students know that they'll have the opportunity to discuss something in the L1 in the future, it can be much easier for them to really *try* during activities in English. After all, most students find it much easier to accept the idea that there's a time and place for the L1, rather than that there's no place for the L1 in the classroom.

A few more important points are:

- Set a time for a clinic (perhaps fifteen or twenty minutes) and *stick to it*! Don't let these activities go on and on. Remember that students need to *practise* English.
- Encourage your students to ask about things connected with what they've been studying. If they simply ask about 'anything they like', then you'll probably get some questions which are about things way beyond their level or things which aren't very important. One example from my own experience is the beginner who asked: *Why is 'I' spelled with a capital letter?* This might be a very interesting question, but most beginners have more important things to worry about!
- Don't worry if you don't know the answer to a question. No teacher knows the answer to every question! And very importantly, if you're a non-native speaker and you don't know the answer to something:

> Don't assume that it's *because* you're a non-native speaker.

It might well be a question that a native speaker teacher couldn't answer either. You can always look the answer up and give it to the students in the next lesson. Or, if you're really worried about this side of things, you can get the students to hand in their questions in advance so that you have time to prepare your answers.

Questions and further activities

1 In the introduction to this book a distinction was made between the L1 (the students' common language in the classroom) and the mother tongue (each student's own first language). These are not always the same; in a class in Moscow the students' mother tongues may include Ukrainian, Georgian, Latvian etc., but the L1 is likely to be Russian. What is the students' L1 in your classes? Is it the same as the mother tongue for all the students? If not, could this be a problem and how can you best deal with it?
2 In this chapter we compared learning a foreign language to learning to play a musical instrument. Is this a good comparison? In what ways are the two processes similar and different?
3 Think back to when you were learning English. How much use was made of the L1 in your classes? Was it used appropriately?
4 In addition to level, stage of the course and stage of the lesson, can you think of any other factors which should influence how much L1 is used in the classroom?

References

1 *Visuals for the Language Classroom* by Andrew Wright and Safia Haleem (Longman 1991)
2 *Mistakes and Correction* by Julian Edge (Longman 1989)

The role of the L1 in presenting and practising new language

The importance of presentation and practice

Presenting and giving controlled practice in new language are two of the teacher's most important jobs. Why is this? Students obviously need to learn new language items in order to make progress. *What* they learn will often be a question of what's in the syllabus and the syllabus will often be in the textbook. In the case of new language, the main concern of most teachers will be *how* to present the new items to the students and how to give them sufficient practice. The students must understand the new language item and they need to practise it in order to be able to use it.

Grammatical form, meaning and the L1

The teacher needs to make sure that the students know about the grammatical form of the new item, its pronunciation and how to use it. In other words, when presenting new language the teacher needs to focus on at least two important aspects of it:

- Form
- Meaning.

Form
To take an example, what are the main difficulties which students may have with *the present continuous* when used in the following way?

I'm having lunch with Florentino next Friday.

The students may have different kinds of problems depending on whether their L1 has any continuous tenses or not. But there are a number of key points about the form of this tense which most teachers will need to bear in mind. For example, at some point, the students will need to know that questions are made by inverting the subject and the verb, as in *Is she enjoying the visit?*, not *She's enjoying the visit?* If they've already learned *the present simple*, they may also need reminding that the negative is formed without *doesn't/don't* (*She isn't enjoying it*). And so on.

> ACTIVITY
>
> Make a list of other problems which in your experience learners tend to have with the form of *the present continuous*.

Meaning
This will be a real problem for many learners, because English is very unusual in having a *present continuous* tense which can be used (sometimes!) to refer to the future. Many students find it very difficult to understand and accept that this is one of the most common ways in which native speakers talk about the future.

Form and meaning are equally as important in vocabulary as in grammar teaching. To take another example, what are the most important aspects of a word like *furniture*?

Form
It is essential that students know that *furniture* is an *uncountable* noun; that is, you can't say things like *a nice furniture* or *some expensive furnitures*. Again, the students' L1 is relevant here; there are many languages in which the 'equivalent' of *furniture* is *countable*. It's also very important for them to know that *furniture* has three syllables and that the stress is on the first one (*FURniture*).

Meaning
The idea of furniture has an appropriate 'equivalent' in many languages. However, the teacher will need to make sure that the students understand what sort of things *furniture* is. It may also be necessary to check whether or not the students are translating the word correctly. (Many learners will translate things for themselves, whether the teacher thinks this is a good thing or not.)

> ACTIVITY
>
> Look at the following grammar and vocabulary items and decide what are the most important points about their form and meaning for your students, bearing in mind the students' L1.
>
> - He can swim. (*can* used for ability)
> - I've got a dog. (*have got* used for possession)
> - comfortable
> - actually
>
> You may find it helpful to refer to *Longman English Grammar* by L. G. Alexander (Longman 1988) and/or the *Longman Dictionary of Contemporary English* when doing this activity. Also, another very useful source, describing the problems of learners from a variety of L1 backgrounds, is *Learner English* by Michael Swan and Bernard Smith (Cambridge 1987).

Understanding a new item is not, of course, enough. The students also need controlled and freer practice in getting their tongues round it and using it. If students don't get enough practice in the language, they may end up *knowing* quite a lot *about* English but not being able to *say* very much.

We're now going to look at some techniques which are frequently used in presenting and giving controlled practice in new language. Then we're going to examine the question of when L1 use might be appropriate during these stages of a lesson.

Some common presentation and practice techniques

Concha Fernández, a teacher of young Spanish learners, is going to introduce one of her groups of elementary students to the present simple tense. The students' coursebook presents the forms of this tense through the situation of the everyday lives of some dolphins and their trainers:

Example 1

A DAY IN THE LIFE OF
Joe Trounson

Joe Trounson trains dolphins. A typical day starts at 8am. Joe checks that the water is clean and the correct temperature, then prepares the dolphins' food. Each dolphin eats about 4.5 kg of fish a day. At 10am Joe starts the training.

'I usually swim with them for a while before the first show,' says Joe. 'I always give them fish if they are good.'

During the show the dolphins do a lot of tricks. They jump out of the water, swim backwards on their tails, and take fish out of Joe's mouth. Joe sometimes rides on a dolphin like a horse!

Joe doesn't work alone. His friend Carol helps him with the training and the shows. 'We work as a team,' says Carol. 'Joe, myself, and the dolphins – Honey, Lulu, Smartie, Cookie and Snappie.'

Joe and Carol finish work at 7pm, but they don't usually go home until much later. If a dolphin is ill, they stay at the pool and talk to the vet.

'It's hard work, but I enjoy it,' says Joe. 'Dolphins are lovely animals to work with.'

Concha has decided to use a similar situation for oral presentation and practice. During this, the students keep their books closed. She often uses many of the following techniques for presentation and practice of new language:

- drill(s)
- listening stage
- games
- eliciting language
- checking comprehension
- lead-in
- correction
- creativity stage
- personalisation

You may not be familiar with all of these techniques, so what follows is a 'matching exercise' to help clarify exactly what they are.

Below are nine parts of Concha's lesson(s) on *the present simple*. Each of the parts includes an example of one of the techniques which she often uses. Beside each part there's a box; decide which of the nine techniques is being demonstrated and write the name of the technique in the box. For example, if you think that number 1 is the lead-in, write *lead-in* in the box, as below:

1 Right, everyone (holding up a visual of a dolphin). What's this? Yes, Roberto? Yes, it's a dolphin.

Now do the matching activity;

1 Right, everyone (holding up a visual of a dolphin). Do you know what this is? Yes, it's a dolphin.

2 Okay, can someone tell me about where dolphins live? Yes, Julia? Yes, in the sea. Can you make that into a sentence?

3 Yes, that's it, Julia. Listen, everyone ... are you listening, Paco? Good. Listen everyone ... (teacher repeats 'Dolphins live in the sea' several times).

4 Can you all repeat that? Good, again. Again. Rita ... okay. Guillermo ... yes. José María ... okay. (etc.)

5 Fernando ... (Fernando says 'Dolphin live in the sea'.) Well, Fernando, is it singular or plural? Yes, plural, so ... yes, that's right, good.

6 Now, how do you say 'Dolphins live in the sea' in Spanish? Josefina? Yes, that's right.

Later in the lesson ...

7 Right, we've talked about where dolphins live, what they eat, and so on. Now I want you to make up a few sentences about you. (Individually, students make up a few sentences such as 'I live in Madrid'.)

Later in the lesson, after the teacher has introduced the third person 's' form ('he/she/it lives' etc.).

8 Now I want you, in pairs, to make up five sentences about Spiderman (or another character, depending on the students' interests). (Students make up sentences like 'Spiderman lives in New York' etc.)

In another lesson, after the students have learned and practised question forms in the present simple.

9 Right, I'm thinking of a famous person. You can ask me 'yes/no' questions to find out who it is. You can ask up to twenty questions. (Students ask questions like 'Does he live in Moscow? Is he a politician?' etc.)

Do you agree with the following 'solution' ?:

1 = lead-in	6 = checking comprehension
2 = eliciting language	7 = personalisation
3 = listening stage	8 = creativity stage
4 = drill(s)	9 = games
5 = correction	

How many of these techniques do you use regularly? (In some cases, you may already use a technique but not be familiar with the name that I've given it here.) These nine techniques are used quite often by many teachers, frequently in the order given here. We're now going to look at each of them in more detail, as we discuss the role of the L1 in presentation and practice of new language.

The role of the L1

The purpose of presentation and practice is to show the students how a new piece of language works and to give them opportunities to begin using it. Obviously, this can only be done efficiently if English is the principal language used by the students and the teacher. However, at low levels especially, the L1 can sometimes be useful.

In the table below, put a tick under 'Yes' or 'No', according to whether you think use of the L1 could be appropriate or not in the case of that particular technique.

Stage	Yes	No
lead-in		
eliciting language		
giving instructions		
checking comprehension		
listening stage		
drill(s)		
correction		
personalisation		
creativity stage		
games		

We'll now look at the techniques one by one. (My own 'solution' is on page 36.)

Lead-ins

It may be useful to exploit the L1 to check that the students have understood the situation. For example,

T: Who can tell me where dolphins live?
  Can you tell me in Spanish?

S: 'Dolphins live in the sea' *(in L1)*

Or, sometimes teachers might want to explain some things in the L1 themselves. Obviously, it's better if it can all be done in English, but there are two very important points about lead-ins:

- They should be *quick*. The important thing is the new language item. It doesn't make sense to spend a long time building up a situation exclusively in English and then find that you don't have enough time to present and practise the language properly. The L1 can help here.
- The students *must* understand the situation. Although lead-ins

need to be quick, it's vital that the students understand what's going on *before* they begin practising. Otherwise, the practice won't be very efficient, the students may become confused or bored and with children you may be faced with discipline problems. It can be a good idea, therefore, to use the L1 a little in order to avoid such problems.

Eliciting language

Eliciting means getting language *from* the students, if possible, rather than giving it *to* them. It is a very useful technique as it increases student participation, and gives the students the opportunity to show what they know. It also gives you, the teacher, a better idea of which students know what (this is especially useful in mixed level classes). There are lots of ways of eliciting. For example, to elicit vocabulary you can use:

- a picture
- a drawing
- the actual object
- mime.

But, if none of these work, you can use the L1 to elicit the word you want from the students. For example,

T: How do you say .... in English?
                    (word in L1)
S: ....
   (word in English)

As always, the L1 should be used sparingly, but eliciting *is* a powerful technique. It's certainly better to elicit through the L1 than not at all.

Giving instructions

Like lead-ins, instructions need to be quick and clear. Very frequently, techniques such as gesture and mime can help to make it possible to give concise instructions in English. But, again, there's not much point in spending for example five minutes giving the instructions for an activity which is going to last seven minutes (or perhaps even three minutes!). For this reason, you may wish to give instructions in the L1 for, say, a complicated communicative activity. In fact, at lower levels there are some good activities which it would be very difficult to set up without using the L1. There are some examples of this in the section later on personalisation, creativity and games. A useful 'halfway' stage is to give the instructions in English and get a good student to summarise them in the L1. This will confirm for you that the good student has understood, and it may clarify things for any weaker students who hadn't understood the English version completely.

It's also important to note that sometimes instructions which can be given in English in the classroom might need the help of the L1 if they're given in written form on a worksheet or in a textbook.

ACTIVITY

A The following exercises are taken from unit 6 of a course for Italian beginners, and are designed to be used as homework. As you can see, the instructions are in Italian (I've added English translations for this activity). Are these instructions in the L1 necessary and/or helpful? What arguments are there for and against including L1 instructions in written materials?

Example 2

Would you be able to manage in English in the following situations?

3 **Jane, la tua corrispondente inglese, ti ha chiesto nella sua ultima lettera:**	3 Jane, your English penfriend, has asked you in her last letter:
1. se sai nuotare 2. se sei capace di usare un computer.	1. if you can swim 2. if you know how to use a computer
Che cosa le risponderesti?	How would you reply?
....	....
4 **Che domande faresti a Chris per sapere:**	4 What questions would you ask Chris to find out:
1. se sa suonare la chitarra?	1. if he can play the guitar
....	....
2. se sua sorella Jane sa il francese?	2. if his sister Jane can speak French
....	....

5 Chris ti ha chiesto della frutta. Hai solo delle banane e delle arance. Che domande gli faresti per sapere cosa preferisce?	5 Chris has asked you for some fruit. You've only got some bananas and some oranges. What would you ask to find out what he prefers? ....
6 L'insegnante di inglese ha pronunciato il nome di una città americana a te sconosciuta. Come gli/le chiederesti di scandire questo nome?	6 The English teacher has said the name of an American city which you don't know. How would you ask him or her to say the name clearly? ....

The basic point about using the L1 in written instructions is the same as the more general point that the L1 is a resource (one of many), to be used only when needed. So if instructions can be written in English in a way in which students can understand them, then there's no point in using the L1.

Would it be possible to use English in the case of our example? It seems to me that it would be, at least some of the time. Do you think students at this level would be able to understand the following version of the instructions, written in English, with a few words translated into Italian?

---

3 Jane, your English penfriend, has asked you two questions in a letter.

Can you swim?

Do you know how to use a computer?

What do you reply?

4 You want to know if Chris can play the guitar.

What question can you ask?

You also want to know if his sister, Jane, can speak French?

What question can you ask this time?

5 Chris wants some fruit. You've only got bananas and oranges. Ask him what he prefers.

6 Your English teacher says the name of an American city, but you don't understand. Ask him to say the name more clearly.

Would students understand these instructions? Probably. But by giving them the instructions in English, we give them a lot of the words which they need in the exercise and perhaps make the activity less challenging. The L1 version forces the students to find the words that they need in English, whereas the English version gives them the words (to a large extent), which they then have to manipulate. Is this a disadvantage? What do you think? Is this a case where the L1 is justified?

B If you have materials which use L1 instructions, try rewriting some of them in English yourself. Is it possible? Does it create the same problem as in part A?

Checking comprehension

There are many techniques which can be used to check whether or not students understand a word or phrase. Here are some of them:

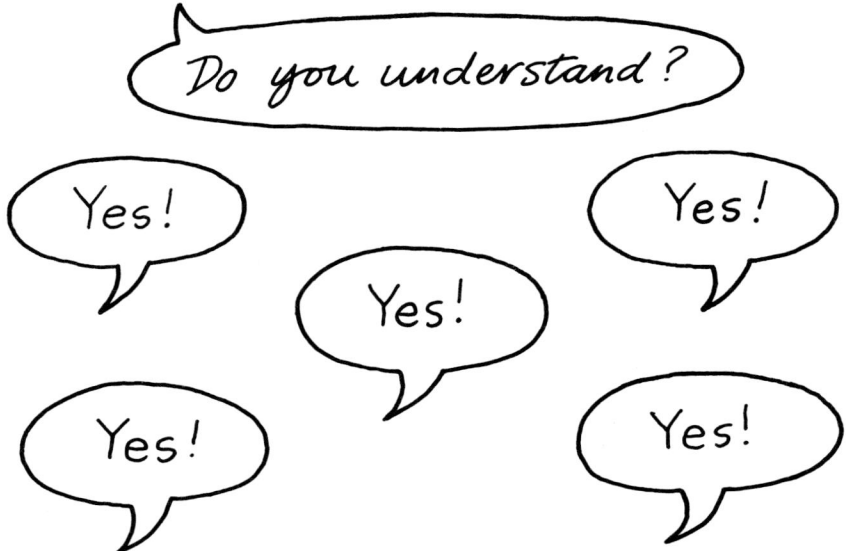

'Do you understand?'

This is not usually the best technique to use, because students can simply reply 'yes' whether they've understood or not.

Concept questions

This is a very useful technique. The teacher asks questions whose answers show whether or not the students have really understood. For example,

Language item	Question(s)	Correct answer(s)
He went to London. (*past simple*)	*Present or past?*	Past.
He's been playing the guitar for 5 years. (*present perfect continuous*)	*When did it begin?* *Has it finished?*	5 years ago. No.
a telephone box	*What's in it?* *Where is it?*	A phone. In the street.
embarrassed	*Is she happy?* *Is she angry?*	No. No.
	What colour is her face?	Red
	Why?	Because she's

ACTIVITY

Design concept questions for the following items:

- Venice is sinking into the sea. (*present continuous*)
- a widow
- a newsagent's
- luxurious

Asking for a definition

T: Which animals can you see at the zoo?
S: Giraffes.
T: Good. What's a giraffe?
S: It's a big animal with a long neck ... etc.

Definitions can be useful, but there is often a problem. Giving a definition is frequently very difficult even in your own language, so it may be that the student does understand but simply can't define the word.

Translation

Concept questions and definitions, while very useful in some cases, can be time-consuming. There are occasions when the simplest, clearest way of checking whether the students have understood something is to get them to think of a translation of it. This is dealt with in more detail in the section of this chapter on 'getting meaning across'.

Listening stage

At this stage of a presentation, the purpose is to give the students the opportunity to listen carefully to the new language item and to begin to assimilate its meaning. The teacher says the first example several times and the students listen in silence; this means that the students can really hear the language before trying to repeat it themselves. As a rule, use of the L1 at this stage is inappropriate and should be avoided since it would be distracting and might break the students' concentration.

Drills

A good drill gives students intensive, controlled practice. Drills help students to assimilate and remember language and, far from being boring, can be fun. In order to exploit drills efficiently, however, it's very important that they should be fairly short and done at a brisk, lively pace, so that the students get a lot of practice and don't have time to get bored. Use of the L1 at this stage would slow things down and interfere with the important rhythm of the drill. So, again, it is best avoided.

Note: Chapter 4 of Donn Byrne's *Techniques for Classroom Interaction* (in this series) describes many different kinds of interesting drills.

Correction

There are many ways of correcting students' mistakes and encouraging students to correct themselves. For example, to encourage correction of a sentence like:

What time he get up yesterday?

the teacher might say any of the following:

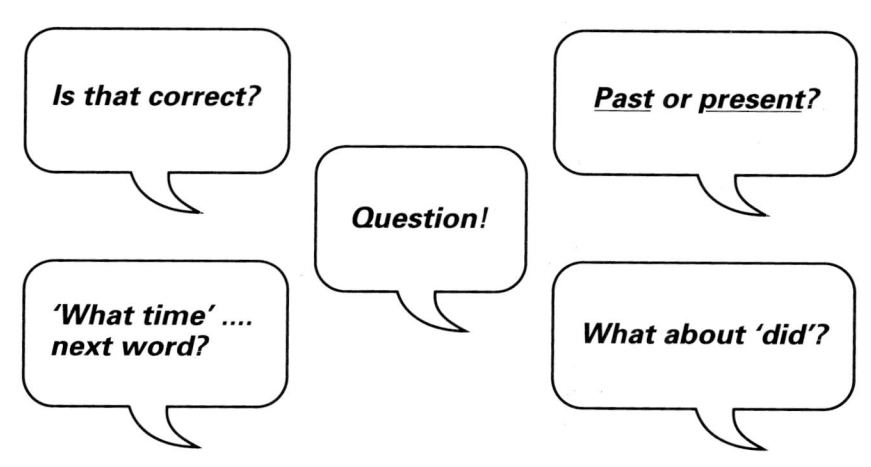

> **Is that correct?**

> **Past or present?**

> **Question!**

> **'What time' .... next word?**

> **What about 'did'?**

Or, depending on the circumstances, the teacher might simply give the correct version and ask the student(s) to repeat it. In any case, the L1 is usually unnecessary for the purposes of correction. However, it can of course be very useful to refer to the L1 to help a student to *understand* a word or a structure which is causing confusion.

Note: Julian Edge's book *Mistakes and Correction* (in this series) discusses a large number of aspects of correction.

Personalisation

Personalisation means bringing the students' own lives into the lesson in a meaningful way, by making the students themselves the 'topic' of an activity. For example, during practice of the structure *used to*, the teacher might get the students to tell each other about things which they used to (and didn't used to) do. This helps to increase the students' involvement in the lesson and the language; after all, most people find their own lives an interesting subject for conversation! It also helps to reinforce the fact that the L2 is a real, living language.

Creativity stage

The creativity stage is simply a part of a presentation where learners are encouraged to use *original* examples of the language which they're practising. For example, in the case of *the present continuous for the future* (which we discussed at the beginning of this chapter) the teacher might get the students to do a role play with role cards like these:

Jane	Paul
You really don't want to see Paul next weekend. When he phones you, make excuses if he suggests doing anything at the weekend. You'll need a different excuse for each suggestion.	You really want to see Jane next weekend. When you phone her, suggest different things you could do next weekend. You should have at least three or four suggestions.

The idea is that the students then have conversations in pairs, using phrases such as *Are you doing anything on Friday evening?*
– *Well, actually, I'm ...* etc.

Like personalisation, creativity stages help to get the learners more involved in what's going on. In addition to this, they're particularly useful for helping learners to remember language – a sentence which you invent yourself is much more memorable than one which the teacher tells you to say. They can also enable the teacher to find out whether the students have really understood and learned something. For instance, if in the *used to* activity a student who is a keen football fan says *I used to watch football matches*, then the teacher can be fairly sure that that particular student hasn't understood the structure *used to*!

Games

Games also allow learners to be creative with the language and to use it in meaningful, communicative ways. Also, perhaps most importantly, they offer learners an opportunity to have fun and to relax in the classroom, while getting useful practice in English at the same time. Games can be a very significant element in a balanced, communicative approach to language practice. Here is another example of a game, which many teachers find useful for practising verb forms in an enjoyable way:

Example 3

> ### 22 Coffeepotting
>
> | | |
> |---|---|
> | *Aims* | *Skills* – speaking |
> | | *Language* – questions, giving evasive answers |
> | | *Other* – fun |
> | *Level* | Beginners/intermediate |
> | *Organisation* | Two groups of different sizes (one group should have one third of the total number of students, the other, two thirds) |
> | *Preparation* | Chairs arranged in two rows facing each other |
> | *Time* | 10–15 minutes |
> | *Procedure* | *Step 1:* The groups sit down facing one another. Then the teacher, without letting the others see it, shows all the members of the smaller group a piece of paper with an activity (e.g. reading or skiing) written on it. |
> | | *Step 2:* The members of the bigger group now have to guess this activity. In their questions they use the substitute verb 'to coffeepot', e.g. 'Is coffeepotting fun in winter?' Both yes/no questions and wh-questions are allowed, but not the direct question 'What is coffeepotting?' The students in the smaller group are allowed to give evasive answers, though they should be basically correct. Each person in the smaller group is questioned by two members of the other group. |
> | | *Step 3:* As soon as a student from the guessing group thinks he has found the solution, he whispers it to the teacher and – if correct – joins the answering group. The game is finished when the original numbers of the groups (1/3 to 2/3) have been reversed. |

Personalisation, creativity stages and games are designed, like drills, to give intensive practice of the L2, so again L1 use should be minimal. However, as we said earlier, instructions may need to involve L1 use. A good example is *Example 3* 'Coffeepotting'; some students find it very difficult to understand that *coffeepotting* is not a real word and a quick, clear L1 explanation of how the game works can be very useful.

It also often happens at this stage that students want to ask questions like:

How do you say 'x' in English?

For example, in a game like 'Twenty questions', where a student must guess what/who another person is thinking about by asking questions, a student might want to ask something like *Did he write novels?* and will ask the teacher how to say *novels* in English.

Sometimes it may be a good idea to give the student the translation into English that he or she wants, but in general it's probably better to encourage students to find another way of saying the same thing (how about *books* instead of *novels*?) or, to think of something that they *can* say in English. Too many interruptions for translations will slow down the activity and possibly defeat its purpose.

Another reason for not allowing students to ask too many questions of this kind is that it is important that students get used to expressing themselves with the English that they *do* know. It is a question of finding a balance between frustrating the students by not giving them the exact words that they want and encouraging them to be 'lazy' by never making them work hard to express themselves with the English which they do have.

> Learners need to understand and accept that they'll *never* have all the words 'at their fingertips' – we all have to express ourselves as best we can, even in our own language!

ACTIVITY

My 'solution', then, to the question of the L1 in presentation and practice is as below. Do you agree with it? Why (not)?

Stage	Yes	No
lead-in	✓	
eliciting language	✓	
giving instructions	✓	
checking comprehension	✓	
listening stage		✓
drill(s)		(✓)*
correction		(✓)
personalisation		(✓)
creativity stage		(✓)
games		(✓)
*(✓) under *No* means 'not usually'		

Getting meaning across

When presenting new language, it's obviously essential that the meaning of the words is clear to the students. Some techniques often used for this purpose were mentioned in the previous section, such as giving definitions and using board drawings.

The purpose of this section is to consider this question in more detail, particularly as regards the use of translation.

ACTIVITY

A Make a list of techniques which you have used, or are familiar with, for making the meanings of words clear to students.

B Now compare your list with the list below:
- drawing;
- mime;
- translation;
- giving an example;
- a picture or photo;
- using an object from outside e.g. an umbrella;
- a facial expression e.g. for *sad*;
- a hand gesture e.g. *to stop*;
- a classroom object e.g. a chair;
- the teacher or students themselves e.g. for a part of the body;
- giving definition;
- through a text – the students read a text and guess the meanings of the new words.

C Now think about each of the following words and phrases and decide which technique would be most appropriate for communicating its meaning to a group of students.

to stare	to crawl	to dive
upside down	tired	worried
a cat	a lizard	a badger
foot	toes	ankle
a tin opener	a window frame	a vehicle

Obviously, there isn't always one, single, 'correct' solution in an activity like this, but we can make a few points.

1 Translation is best kept for situations where other, more direct techniques are inappropriate. Before using translation, teachers need to ask themselves questions such as:

- *Is it easy to draw?*
- *Could I mime it?*
- *Is it in the classroom?*
  and so on.

2 There's not much point in using translation to get across the meaning of a word like *boat, smile* or *pencil sharpener* when this can be done more easily by means of, for instance, a visual, mime or reference to an object in the classroom. It's important that students develop the ability to understand and learn English through English. There are many cases in which the meanings of words can be clarified without the use of any translation.

3 Learners need to be made aware that if the teacher uses translation to get the meaning of something across, the translation given is valid *for that particular context*. It doesn't mean that the learner can necessarily translate the word back into English in other contexts. For example, if a Spanish learner knows that *fresh*, as in *fresh fish* translates as 'fresco', he or she shouldn't assume that the phrase *Hace fresco*, used of the weather, can be translated as 'It's fresh', since it means something more like *It's not very warm*.

4 Translation can only be used where an accurate translation exists. There are many cases where a word can't be translated from one language into another satisfactorily.

5 There isn't always *one* most appropriate way of clarifying meaning; it often depends on circumstances, resources, the individual teacher, etc. It can be very useful to combine techniques, so as to be as certain as possible that the students will understand. In particular, translation can sometimes be a good way of checking that the students have really understood a word that has been taught in the L2. After all, visuals, information about context, mime, etc. aren't foolproof.

Further issues connected with translation are dealt with in chapter 5. In the next chapter we will look at aspects of pair and group work in monolingual classes.

Questions and further activities

1 Do you think that *the present continuous for future arrangements* is most difficult for students whose L1 has *continuous* forms or for those whose L1 has no *continuous* tenses at all? Are the forms in another language which are most different from our L1 always the ones which we find most difficult?
2 Do you use all the 'stages of presentation' described at the beginning of this chapter? If not, choose three of the ones you haven't used before, which you think would work in your classes, and try them out in one or two of your next presentations.
3 How much of the students' L1 do you use in presentation and controlled practice? Try to pay attention to this in two or three of your next classes and then ask yourself: *Do I use the L1 too much? Are there any stages at which I could use it less?*
4 Think of a recent example where you gave an explanation or instruction in English which you feel was unsatisfactory. Why was this? Did it take too long? Did the students fail to understand? What would have helped make it clearer?
5 Do you think that there are stronger arguments for using written L1 instructions in homework materials or teaching materials?
6 Make a list of ten vocabulary items whose meaning you feel can best be communicated by translation. Why is it that translation is the best technique in each case?

References

1 *Longman English Grammar* by L.G. Alexander (Longman 1988)
2 *Longman Dictionary of Contemporary English* (Longman 1987)
3 *Learner English* by Michael Swan and Bernard Smith (Cambridge 1987)
4 *Techniques for Classroom Interaction* by Donn Byrne, chapter 4 (Longman 1987)
5 *Mistakes and Correction* by Julian Edge (Longman 1989)
6 *Example 1* from *World Class* by Michael Harris and David Mower (Longman 1991)
7 *Example 2* from *Flying Start Activity Book* by Steve Elsworth and Luciano Mariana (Longman Italia 1987)
8 *Example 3* from *Keep Talking* by Friederike Klippel (Cambridge 1984)

4 Pair and group work in monolingual classes

It is sometimes said that it is easier to use pair and group work in multilingual classes because the students can *only* communicate with each other in English, whereas in monolingual classes they could just as easily speak to each other in their L1. Whether this is true or not, it certainly is true that in monolingual classes pair and group activities need to be chosen carefully and set up in appropriate ways. The purpose of this chapter is to examine some ways of helping to make a success of pair and group work in monolingual classes of any size.

The importance of pair and group work

But why use pair and group work at all? Below are some of the reasons for using this kind of activity, first from the learners' point of view then from the teacher's.

The learners

- *Practice* ... Learners get a lot more practice. In a class of forty during a teacher-led activity only one person is speaking at any one time, whereas during pair work twenty people are speaking.
- *Confidence* ... It can feel much more comfortable to speak in a foreign language to just one or two people, rather than to the whole class and the teacher. And after all, speaking to just a couple of people is much closer to most 'real-life' situations.
- *Pace* ... Pair and group work allows each student to work at the pace of his or her own small group or pair. This is likely to be

nearer each individual's own 'ideal' pace of work than in activities where the teacher sets the pace for the whole class.
- *Ways of learning* ... The learners can learn from each other; the teacher isn't the only person in the classroom who the students can learn from. Every learner knows different things and learns in different ways; pair and group work creates opportunities for learners' knowledge to be shared.
- *Independence* ... In order to be successful, learners need to become accustomed to using English without the teacher always looking on. Pair and group activities can help them to do this.

The teacher

- *Time* ... Pair and group work gives the teacher more time to work with weaker students. It also allows the teacher a little time to step back for a moment in order to consult a lesson plan, organise materials for the next stage of a lesson, reflect on how things are going, etc. Being the focus of attention for every minute of a lesson is extremely demanding and it certainly isn't usually the best way of teaching.
- *Variety* ... There are many types of activity which work best in pairs or small groups. This is especially true of many 'communicative' types of activity, such as games, role plays, discussions etc.
- *Feedback* ... Pair and group activities give the teacher valuable feedback on how well the students are learning. If, for example, a class have recently learned the past simple, they can do a pair work activity on this while the teacher moves around the class listening in to the pairs. This feedback will help the teacher to decide whether any 'remedial' work is necessary in this area.

Perhaps the most important of all these factors is that pair and group activities give more students more practice more of the time. One 'common sense' truth about language learning is that in order to make progress, you *must* practise as much as possible.

Organising a class for pair and group work

Pair and group work can be used in almost any teaching situation, even in large classes where the furniture is fixed to the floor.

In the first figure on the next page, a class of thirty-six students is divided into eighteen pairs.

Fig. 1

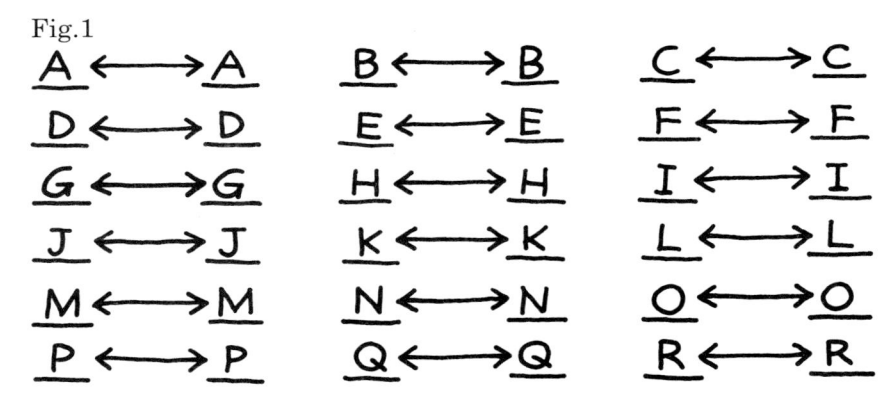

```
A ←→ A      B ←→ B      C ←→ C
D ←→ D      E ←→ E      F ←→ F
G ←→ G      H ←→ H      I ←→ I
J ←→ J      K ←→ K      L ←→ L
M ←→ M      N ←→ N      O ←→ O
P ←→ P      Q ←→ Q      R ←→ R
```

In the second figure, the same class of thirty-six students is divided into nine groups of four. If the furniture in the classroom can't be moved, then the students in rows one, three and five may need to turn round to face the students behind them.

Fig. 2

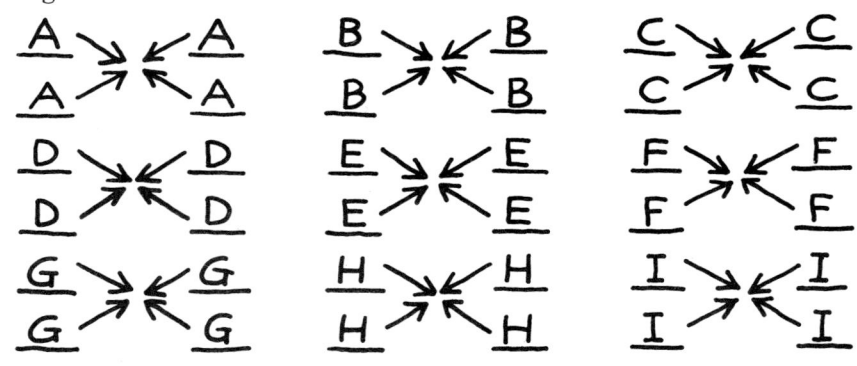

```
A ↘ ↙ A      B ↘ ↙ B      C ↘ ↙ C
A ↗ ↖ A      B ↗ ↖ B      C ↗ ↖ C

D ↘ ↙ D      E ↘ ↙ E      F ↘ ↙ F
D ↗ ↖ D      E ↗ ↖ E      F ↗ ↖ F

G ↘ ↙ G      H ↘ ↙ H      I ↘ ↙ I
G ↗ ↖ G      H ↗ ↖ H      I ↗ ↖ I
```

Making pair and group activities work

The success of any pair or group activity depends to a large extent on:

- *Preparation* ... Are the students well enough prepared? Do they know what to say? Can they say it in English, etc.?
- *Level* ... Is the activity at the right level of difficulty?
- *Appropriacy* ... Is it an appropriate kind of activity?
- *The teacher* ... Does the teacher organise it properly?

We'll take these factors one by one and look at some sample activities.

Preparation

In any pair or group activity, whether it comes from a textbook or a resource book or is the teacher's own idea, it's essential that the students have a clear, limited task to carry out. In most cases *Talk about x or y* isn't enough. The activity must be clearly structured and, before it begins, the teacher needs to check that everyone knows exactly what they have to do.

In addition to this, the teacher needs to be sure that the students actually do know and can use the structures, vocabulary etc. which they need. Pair and group work is much more demanding than just listening to the teacher or repeating some phrases during a drill. If a pair or group activity doesn't work very well, one of the most common reasons is that the students haven't had sufficient practice beforehand. This applies particularly to controlled practice, but there are also many freer activities (games, role plays, etc.) for which students will need, say, certain key vocabulary items before they begin.

Level

Activities of any kind in the classroom must be of approximately the correct level. If an activity is too difficult, then the students may become discouraged and lose interest. On the other hand, activities which are too easy will not challenge the students and they may lose interest for this reason. In general:

> An activity is at the right level if it is challenging for the students but *most* of them can do it with *some* success *most* of the time.

> ACTIVITY
>
> Think carefully about one of the levels which you teach most frequently. Look at each of the following activities and decide whether your students, at the level which you've chosen, would have the necessary *language* to be able to do the activity reasonably successfully. (We'll discuss how *appropria*te the activities are in the next section.)

Example 1

B Work with a partner to decide on one sentence for each picture beginning with *You shouldn't . . .*

Example: You shouldn't go to bed late every day.

1 You shouldn't ⎯⎯⎯⎯⎯⎯⎯⎯⎯⎯⎯⎯⎯⎯⎯⎯⎯⎯⎯⎯⎯⎯⎯
2 You shouldn't ⎯⎯⎯⎯⎯⎯⎯⎯⎯⎯⎯⎯⎯⎯⎯⎯⎯⎯⎯⎯⎯⎯⎯
3 You shouldn't ⎯⎯⎯⎯⎯⎯⎯⎯⎯⎯⎯⎯⎯⎯⎯⎯⎯⎯⎯⎯⎯⎯⎯
4 You shouldn't ⎯⎯⎯⎯⎯⎯⎯⎯⎯⎯⎯⎯⎯⎯⎯⎯⎯⎯⎯⎯⎯⎯⎯
5 You shouldn't ⎯⎯⎯⎯⎯⎯⎯⎯⎯⎯⎯⎯⎯⎯⎯⎯⎯⎯⎯⎯⎯⎯⎯
6 You shouldn't ⎯⎯⎯⎯⎯⎯⎯⎯⎯⎯⎯⎯⎯⎯⎯⎯⎯⎯⎯⎯⎯⎯⎯

Compare sentences with two other students.

C Perhaps it's just a question of doing these things too often or too much. Work in groups of three or four to decide what limits you could put on each of the activities in the pictures.

Example: Lying in the sun is okay, but not for the whole day.

Example 2

4 Work in groups of three or four. In each group, choose one of the following subjects. Prepare some more questions. When your questionnaire is ready, go round the class asking your questions. Note the answers. Then report to the class on what people think. Give your own opinions as well.

FRIENDSHIP
How important are your friends to you?
....

LOVE AND SEX
Do you think you can love more than one person at the same time?
....

MARRIAGE
Do you think marriage is a good thing?
....

PARENT–CHILD RELATIONSHIPS
Do you think most children can communicate well with their parents?
....

HOMOSEXUAL RELATIONSHIPS
Do you think homosexual relationships are wrong?
....

RELATIONSHIPS IN WORK AND SOCIETY
Do you ever start conversations with strangers?
....

Example 3

Procedure

1 Ask learners to walk around the room looking at things. When they see something they know the name of in English, they say the name out loud. So learners go around muttering *table ... carpet ... friend ... shirt ... view*, etc. This is a simple review of known vocabulary items.
2 Next ask learners to do the same thing except that they 'share' their word. When they see something they know the name of, they touch another learner on the arm, point to the thing to be named and name it out loud. The person listening then returns the favour by pointing to something else and naming it out loud too. This way vocabulary that one learner knows can be transferred to another.
3 Now for the hilarious part! From now on, learners go around the room spotting things, tapping each other on the arm, pointing to the object to be named and calling out the WRONG name for it! Thus one learner will point at the carpet and shout out, *Ceiling!* Their partner will point to their own nose and say, *Ear*, and so on. At this point laughter will break out, voices will get louder and naming will get more and more outrageous. Soon pairs of learners will come up to the teacher, point and say things like, *Alligator*, burst into fits of laughter and walk away!

Example 4

CONNECTIONS 2

Find the matching pictures.

For example:

Now write a sentence.

I went to the estate agent's to look for a house.

look for   have   buy   book   post   borrow   catch
see   cash

Appropriacy

In general, if you're thinking of using a pair or group activity with a class, you should be able to answer 'yes' to questions like the following ones. If you can't do this, then you may well need to adapt the activity or choose a different one.

- *Is the topic of the activity culturally acceptable?*
  Alcohol and drinking, for instance, are likely to be unsuitable in many cultures. In general, also, it's important not to embarrass students or make them feel uncomfortable by asking them to talk about things which they might feel are too personal.
- *Do the students know enough about the topic?*
  The success of an activity based on the theme of, say, a rock group may depend on how much the students know about the group chosen, or how much information they've been given by the teacher in the course of preparing for the activity.
- *Do the students have the necessary background experience?*
  An activity 'in a restaurant', for instance may not work with students who have never been to a restaurant.
- *Are the students interested in the topic?*
  It's quite possible for students to know a lot about a topic without being particularly interested in it. It's also sometimes possible, of course, for a teacher to stimulate in the students an interest in a certain topic by doing previous activities connected with it.

ACTIVITY

1 Look again at the activities on pages 44 and 45 and ask yourself the above questions.

Are there any activities which would be especially appropriate or inappropriate for your students?

2 Choose three of the activities on pages 44 and 45 and adapt them to make them more suitable for your students.

The teacher

Choosing the right activity is only the beginning. It is also the teacher's job to set up and manage pair and group work in a suitable way. Having chosen an activity and organised the groups or pairs, the teacher must then get things going. Here is a fairly standard procedure which many teachers find works for them quite well. Look at it carefully and then do the activity which follows.

> 1 Give instructions.
> 2 Check instructions.
> 3 Hand out any materials. (In some cases it may not be possible to give clear instructions before the students have seen the materials. But, where possible, this should be done, so that the group's attention has one clear focus at each stage.)
> 4 Get one pair or group to 'demonstrate' the activity before everyone begins.
> 5 Tell all the students to start.
> 6 Wait a very short time and then quickly go round all the groups, making sure that they have all understood what to do and are doing it.
> 7 Go round the pairs or groups, more slowly this time, listening in and making mental notes of errors and other language problems.
> 8 Stop the activity (preferably *before* the students run out of things to say!).
> 9 Check the result of the activity, where appropriate (i.e. if the students have to reach a conclusion, solve a problem etc.).
> 10 Give feedback on the activity. For example, discuss and help them to correct some of the mistakes which they made.

> ACTIVITY
>
> Compare the above procedure with your own approach to pair and group activities. Can you see any ways in which it could help to make activities with your classes as successful as possible?

Note: Two other books in this series – *Effective Class Management* by Mary Underwood and *Techniques for Classroom Interaction* by Donn Byrne – also deal with important aspects of pair and group work.

The role of the L1

We've now looked in detail at setting up appropriate pair and group activities at the right level. Obviously, all of this should be done in English as far as possible. However, in some situations careful, limited use of the L1, at the right time, will help the students to get the maximum possible benefit from an activity.

The activity below will help you to decide what's best in your own situation.

> **ACTIVITY**
>
> Look again at the standard procedure for pair and group work, described on page 47, and decide whether there are any stages in it where the L1 may have a useful role to play. Put a tick or cross by the number of the stage, according to your opinion.
>
> | 1 | 2 | 3 | 4 | 5 |
> |---|---|---|---|----|
> | 6 | 7 | 8 | 9 | 10 |

Now compare your answers with my own comments.

- *Stages 1/2/3/4/5 (giving instructions, etc.):*
  This area was discussed in chapter 3. If instructions can be given efficiently in English, then to use the L1 would simply waste an opportunity to use English in the classroom. However, where the level of the students and/or the type of activity make this difficult, it is sometimes worth either giving or checking the instructions in the L1.

- *Stages 6/7 ('monitoring' what the students are doing):*
  In most circumstances, unless the activity isn't working at all, the teacher's role at this point is to *listen*, not to speak.

  On the other hand, if the activity doesn't seem to be going very well, you may decide to stop the students and use the L1 to find out what the problem is and to clarify things. It's very important to clear things up as quickly as possible in order to keep the rhythm of the activity going. The L1 can be a useful resource to help make sure that no more time than necessary is wasted. In addition to this, students may want to use the L1 to get help in saying specific things in the course of the activity. In this respect, as we said in chapter 3, it's a question of striking a balance between helping and encouraging the students and not spoon-feeding them too much.

- *Stages 8/9/10 (feedback, etc.):*
  As in giving instructions, etc., if feedback can be done in English

there's no point in doing it in the L1. However, some find it useful when explaining and clarifying the student and confusions. It may be, for example, that there are vocabulary where the simplest solution is translation, or area of grammar can be more clearly explained and understood in the L1, or contrasted *with* the L1. An extension of this idea, which we described in chapter 2, is the 'L1 problem clinic'.

One other area which we haven't mentioned is the role of the L1 in discussing with students the purpose of an activity. At lower levels it can be very difficult to talk to the students in English about, for instance, the reasons for doing pair and group work or the importance of fluency activities. In such circumstances, some teachers prefer to introduce a discussion in the L1 rather than have no discussion at all. This area is dealt with in more detail in the section on 'learner training' in chapter 6.

Another point to add is that an 'L1 problem clinic' (see chapter 2) might well involve pair or group work and that this can consist of the students discussing a difficult aspect of English in the L1. This is a perfectly valid activity if it's at a level where the students couldn't do it in English and as long as it doesn't take up too much time.

Dealing with too much L1 use

What if they use the L1 too much?

There *is* a risk of the students using the L1 too much during pair and group work. The next activity describes some of the most common 'L1 problems' and looks at some ways of dealing with them.

If you sometimes feel that your students are using too much L1 unnecessarily, look at the problems in the table and see if you recognise any of them. Then look at the suggested 'remedy' in each case.

1	**Problem**	*The students giggle or look embarrassed or resentful when I ask them to do group or pair work. They don't seem to have any interest in any activities of this kind.*
	Remedy	They may feel self-conscious or silly talking to each other in English. They may not understand the purpose of this kind of work. You may need to talk with them about its importance and explain that any feelings of 'silliness' will disappear with practice. This discussion may well need to take place in the L1.

2	**Problem**	*They just don't seem to feel that pair and group work is worthwhile. They just want to talk in the L1 all the time about anything they feel like.*
	Remedy	Perhaps you're trying to do too much too soon, particularly if you haven't been with the class for very long and don't know them very well. You may need to do fewer, simpler, shorter activities for a while and then slowly build up to more frequent, more complicated and longer activities.
3	**Problem**	*The students seem to spend a lot of time talking in the L1 – about the activity.*
	Remedy	Perhaps they don't know *exactly* what to do. It might be appropriate to stop the activity and check whether they really understand. You may need to clarify how the activity works or provide them with some necessary vocabulary. On the other hand, if they're just checking quickly with each other in the L1, organising who takes which role, etc., this isn't necessarily a problem – as long as they *then* do the activity in English!
4	**Problem**	*The students start off speaking English, but after a while half of them are chatting in the L1.*
	Remedy	Perhaps they've finished! Are you giving them too much time to do some activities? It's easy to overestimate the amount of practice an activity can provide. 'Five minutes', for instance, sounds like quite a short time, but it can be a very long time to spend speaking English if you're an elementary student. Sometimes a more suitable time limit is 'two minutes' or, literally, 'twenty seconds'. *Or* Perhaps the activity is too difficult and the students can't get very far with it. In this case, the teacher needs to consider whether the activity is *really* too difficult or whether the problem is that the students haven't had enough practice and/or preparation.

It's always worth remembering that even if some unnecessary L1 use does take place in a pair or group activity, the majority of the students will probably still use more English than they would be able to during a teacher-led activity. 'Fear of the L1' is not a good reason for avoiding pair and group work!

We've seen that careful use of the L1 at the right time (e.g. discussing methodology in the L1, clarifying instructions through the L1, etc.) can sometimes help to solve the problem of students using the L1 too much in the classroom. Obviously, in this area, as in all others, your decision about which language to use at a particular time will depend on a lot of different factors connected with the students, the materials, yourself, the school, etc. The most important thing is never to lose sight of the fact that:

> English *must* be the main language used in the classroom. That is part of the key to successful teaching!

> ACTIVITY
>
> Choose one of the activities from page 44 or 45 (or your own adaptation of it) and decide exactly how you would set it up. If possible, try it out with one of your own classes.

Conclusion

We've now dealt in a lot of detail with the question of the L1. Before you go on to the second half of the book, consider the following questions:

- Has your view of the role of the L1 changed as a result of working through chapters 1 to 4? If so, in what ways? For example, have you identified any aspects of your teaching in which it would be appropriate for you to use the L1 less, or any ways in which you could make better use of the L1 as a resource?

Note: Further advice on how to use the L2 as much as possible in the classroom is given in *Teaching English Through English* by Jane Willis (Longman 1981) and *On Target* by Susan Halliwell and Barry Jones (Pathfinder Series, CILT 1991). *On Target* is designed for British teachers of other languages, but is nevertheless very useful for English language teachers.

Questions and further activities

1 Think of a lesson which you taught recently, try to write down the different stages which took place in it (or consult your lesson

plan) and then decide whether there are any ways in which you could have integrated more pair and/or group work into it.
2 Make a list of topics and subjects which you think would be inappropriate for pair and group work activities with your students. If possible, get a colleague to do the same and then compare and discuss your lists.
3 On pages 49–50 we looked at some reasons why students might use too much L1 during pair or group work. Can you think of any other possible reasons which we didn't mention? Think of two occasions when your students ended up using the L1 a lot during a pair or group activity. What exactly do you think the reasons for this were in each case?
4 What are the three biggest problems about using group and pair work in your situation? What can you do to overcome or lessen these problems?

References

1 *Effective Class Management* by Mary Underwood (Longman 1987)
2 *Techniques for Classroom Interaction* by Donn Byrne (Longman 1987)
3 *Teaching English through English* by Jane Willis (Longman 1981)
4 *On Target* by Susan Halliwell and Barry Jones (Pathfinder Series, CILT 1991)
5 *Example 1* from *Plenty To Say* by Gaynor Ramsey (Longman 1989)
6 *Example 2* from *The Cambridge English Course Book 3* by Michael Swan and Catherine Walter (Cambridge 1987)
7 *Example 3* from *The Recipe Book* edited by Seth Lindstromberg (Longman 1990)
8 *Example 4* from *Play Games With English 1* by Colin Granger (Heinemann 1980)

Using translation activities

So far in this book, we have looked at the role of the L1 in making various aspects of classroom learning as efficient as possible. In this chapter, we are going to focus on the benefits of using translation itself as a *practice* activity. Translating texts is, like using dialogues, or grammar exercises, or games, another way in which students can practise and learn English. Unlike many other types of practice, however, it is also an activity which can only be fully exploited in monolingual classes.

Some benefits of using translation activities

- Translation forces learners to think carefully about *meaning*, not just to manipulate forms in a way that many 'mechanical' grammar exercises do.
- It allows learners to think *comparatively*. When students do translation activities they have to compare their L1 with English. This can help them to become more aware of the differences between the two languages and to avoid making all sorts of 'typical' mistakes common in their L1 group. Teachers can also choose texts for translation which help the learners to focus on areas which cause them particular difficulty.
- Translation activities can be used to encourage students to *take risks* rather than avoid them. This is useful since sometimes they should be encouraged to 'stretch' their knowledge as far as possible. When translating, you can't look for ways of avoiding saying 'difficult' things; instead, you have to find *some* way of saying them in the other language.
- A brief translation activity is a good way of changing the *pace* of a lesson. If you have just done a lively communicative activity,

following it with some translation can make the focus of the lesson calmer and more reflective.
- Translation is a *real life* activity. If your students need English in their jobs (now or in the future) they may well have to spend some time translating.

Some criticisms of translation

Isn't translation very time-consuming?

Translation has a long history as a very valuable language practice activity. However, for some years now it has been out of fashion in English language teaching. This neglect seems to be partly because of the continual misuse of translation within the classroom. For this reason, we are now going to look at some of the criticisms which are commonly made of translation and comment on their implications for teachers who want to use this technique in a positive and helpful way.

Criticism	Implication for teachers
Translation is boring and it takes up too much class time.	Almost any activity can be interesting or dull – it depends how you use it. There's no need for students to spend large amounts of class time doing individual, silent translation – see the section on translation activities.
Translation focuses on reading and writing, although many students need mainly listening and speaking practice.	It doesn't have to! Some translation activities can be done almost completely as oral activities. And many written activities can be done at home and then discussed in class.
The grammar/translation method isn't very effective.	Very true. Grammar/translation is unsatisfactory for all sorts of reasons. But using translation activities doesn't have to mean using that kind of method. There's no reason why translation shouldn't play a part in a modern, communicative approach.
Translation encourages learners to think in terms of two languages rather than just one (i.e. English).	What's wrong with that? Learners do tend to do this whether the teacher tells them to or not. However, translation should only form a small part of what goes on in the classroom – learners should also have plenty of opportunities to practise English without referring back to the L1.

Translation is a special skill which only professional translators need.	The purpose of translation in the language classroom isn't to produce professional translators. It is to help learners to develop their knowledge of English by giving them opportunities to become more aware of significant differences and similarities between their L1 and English. Teachers should always know why they are using a translation activity and what they expect students to get out of it.
Translation tends to use either difficult literary material or unrealistic invented texts.	Both 'real' and 'made-up' texts have their place. Almost *any* text can be used for translation, from texts written by the teacher or found in the coursebook to road signs, messages, letters, poems, songs, graffiti, etc.

In short, translation activities should and can involve the students in doing interesting things with stimulating material, in ways which use the time available as efficiently as possible.

What is a good translation?

> ACTIVITY
>
> Translate each of the following words and phrases into your own language or into another language if English is your mother tongue, using the best possible translation in each case.
>
> 1 Pleased to meet you.
> 2 I've been living here for ten years.
> 3 Can I have 2 kilos, please?
> 4 In this week's programme, the spotlight is on the problems of public transport.

Was it easy to decide what would be the best translation? Almost certainly not in some cases. In 1, and perhaps 2 and 3, you probably didn't have enough information about the following points in order to translate the phrase with confidence:

- Who's speaking?
- How many people is he/she speaking to?
- Who are they?
- What's the relationship between the people involved?
- Where are they and what are they doing?

Without answers to questions like these, translation can be very difficult or impossible. You simply don't have enough information about the *context*. Teachers should be careful not to put their students in this position:

> Make sure that learners have as much information as they need about context; who is speaking to whom about what and where.

Let's say that in sentence number 1 the speaker is a young man being introduced by his boss to an important visitor. The conversation is taking place at a formal meeting and the young man feels nervous and anxious to make a good impression. Can you translate the sentence now? You may feel there are a number of reasonable possibilities rather than one 'right answer'. That's fine – translation is often about reasonable suggestions, not correct answers.

Context is not the only issue however. In sentence 2 the tense may cause difficulties. You need to find a way of expressing the idea of *the present perfect continuous* here (i.e. a state which began in the past and is still continuing). Learners need to be aware that even if their own language has a *present perfect continuous* form, this may not be the best choice. What we need is a way of expressing the same meaning, *not* a similar form with a different meaning. This is an example of a case where translation can force learners to think about meaning and use, rather than just manipulate forms.

In sentence 3, the point is to find a 'social equivalent' of a polite request (in a shop, for example). As in the case of tenses, equivalence of meaning is more important than using a similar L1 form. The question is: what is *appropriate* in this context? In this case, for instance, few languages would require an L1 form like *Can I have ...?*. German might use a declarative without *please* ('Ich hätte gern ...'), French a declarative with *please* ('Deux kilos de ... s'il vous plaît'), Spanish an imperative ('Déme ...'), and so on.

Sentence 4 raises another point – the idiomatic use of words. Can the 'equivalent' of *spotlight* in your own language be used in the same idiomatic way? If not, how can you best express this idea? Idiomatic, metaphorical language is much more common than many people assume. Learners need to be aware that because two words are 'literal' translation equivalents, this doesn't always mean that they have identical idiomatic uses. To take a random example, the

English *cowboy* is often used nowadays to mean someone who does business in a dishonest or incompetent way, but this obviously isn't true of the 'equivalent' of *cowboy* in most other languages. Equivalence is discussed further in the section on cognates.

We can now summarise some of the things that good translators pay attention to and their implications for teachers:

Good translators	**Implication for teachers**
Pay attention to context.	Make sure your students have as much information as they need about who's saying what to whom, where and why. Help them to understand that in many cases there won't be one 'right' translation of a word – the most appropriate translation will depend on the context.
Concentrate on meaning.	Use translation activities to encourage your students to realise that equivalence of meaning (in a context!) is more important than similarity of form, as in sentence 2 above. Above all, students need to be aware that 'word by word' translation doesn't work most of the time.
Translate 'social' meaning.	Emphasise the importance of social appropriacy. Learners need to understand that often *how* something is said is as important as what is said.
Pay attention to idiomatic language.	Give your students plenty of practice in dealing with this problem. Discuss with them the best ways of translating specific idioms in context.

Note: For further discussion of translation, see *Translation* by Alan Duff (Oxford 1989).

Translation and fluency activities

As well as encouraging learners to 'take risks', translation activities can play a role in helping students to develop confidence in making do with the English which they already know.

How do you say 'x' in English?

One of the potential problems of monolingual classes is that if a student doesn't know a particular word in English there is always someone who can translate it for him or her. This can be useful, of

> *How do you say 'y' in English?*
>
> *How do you say 'z' in English?*

course, but it can also be dangerous. Students who are used to always asking *How do you say x in English?* when they're in any doubt usually find it extremely difficult to communicate efficiently with anyone who doesn't already speak their L1! Teachers who give their students too much help are not really helping them at all.

This problem occurs frequently during communicative fluency activities, when learners get 'stuck' and feel that they simply can't express what they want to in English. Teachers need to find a balance between 'spoon-feeding' and not giving enough help. One useful technique is to get learners to make notes in the L1 of things they 'can't say' in English while they do an activity. At the end, the teacher helps the learners find ways of expressing the items that they noted down in English. For example:

Example Activity

A The teacher sets up a communicative activity in which the students discuss advantages and disadvantages of several different holiday destinations. The students are told that as they do the activity they should note down two or three things which they would like to say but 'can't' say in English.

B The students do the activity in groups. Meanwhile, the teacher 'listens in' to the different groups, making sure that they *are* doing the activity (not discussing in the L1 things that they don't know how to say in English).

C When the students have finished the activity, the teacher elicits from them a selection of, say, ten things (in the L1) which they 'couldn't say' in English. These are written up on the board and the teacher gives the students ten minutes, in groups, to find a way of expressing each of the ideas in English. There are all sorts of strategies that they can use to do this. They might:

- use the opposite of the word which they don't know, e.g. *not difficult* for 'easy', or *Fred lent me the money* for 'I borrowed the money from Fred';
- use a more general or simpler English word than an 'exact' equivalent of the L1 term, e.g. *very unpleasant* for 'disgusting', *very well* for 'fluently', *so* for 'as a result', etc.;
- give a definition of what they mean, e.g. *It's a kind of big bird which can run fast but can't fly* for 'ostrich', or *It's the word for when horses run very fast* for 'gallop', etc.;
- show what they mean, e.g. *She broke her ....* , student points to his or her ankle, etc.

The important thing is that the students are given practice in behaving as if no one else in the room knew their L1; after all, this is the most likely 'real life' situation.

D Each group gives its 'answers' and these are discussed. Afterwards, the teacher can give them the exact English versions of the words, so that next time they'll know them. The main purpose of this technique is to encourage learners *to communicate as much as possible with the English that they know.*

ACTIVITY

Choose a suitable communicative activity and use it with a class, including the above technique.

True cognates and false friends

What are cognates?

The word *cognate* is used to describe a word which has a very similar form in two different languages. Two examples, where several European languages are 'cognate' with English are:

English	*German*	*French*	*Portuguese*	*Italian*
organisation	Organisation	organisation	organização	organizzazione
actual	aktuell	actuel	actual	attuale

We can make two points about these examples:

- *Organisation* is a *true cognate* (a 'true friend'); its form and its meaning are similar to the English. *Actual* is a *false cognate* (or 'false friend'); its form is the same, but its meaning is different. In the languages listed, it means something like 'current' or 'present', which obviously differs from its meaning in English.
- There are obviously far more cognates between English and other European languages than between English and, say, Asian or African languages. However, many languages have at least a few cognates with English.

The role of cognates in learning

For speakers of some languages cognates are an enormously valuable resource – there are huge areas of vocabulary which are much easier to learn because of the similarities between the L1 and English. And even where this isn't true it's still worth encouraging students to be aware of and exploit those cognates which do exist. Some points to bear in mind are:

- Introduce beginners to as many true cognates as possible – this is very good for their confidence.
- Teach students about false cognates – these can cause a lot of problems of mis-translation.
- Encourage learners to guess cognates and give them guidance about the sorts of words which are likely to be 'true friends'. For example, in Spanish many words beginning with *al-* (derived from Arabic) are unlikely to be cognates, whereas many words ending in *-ción* are similar to English words ending in *-tion*.
- On the other hand, learners should be told that where possible they should always check (in a dictionary) to see whether a word really is a true friend before using it. There are surprises in many languages; many Spanish learners visiting the chemist's in English-speaking countries have assumed that *constipado* (meaning 'having a cold') is a true cognate!
- Encourage students to pay attention to pronunciation. This can be a considerable problem, particularly when the L1 has 'borrowed' an English word. Turkish learners, for example, need to realise that *kalite* needs to be pronounced rather differently if an English speaker is to understand it as 'quality'.

In addition to these points, learners need to develop an awareness that there are very few words which are *absolute* true cognates between two languages, i.e. which are exactly the same in all ways. Teachers can encourage students to bear in mind questions such as the following when dealing with 'similar' words:

- *Do the two words mean the same even though they look the same?* That is, are they false friends? For instance *konsento* (Japanese: 'plug'), *sensibile* (Italian: 'sensitive'), *ignorar* (Spanish: 'to not know') are clear examples of words which have completely different meanings in the L1.
- *Do they mean the same in every context?* Almost certainly not. For example, the German *Mutter* means 'mother', except when it means 'nut' (as in 'nuts and bolts'). Or, although the English

word 'key' is an equivalent of the Spanish *llave* in many contexts, Spanish learners need to be aware that it cannot convey the idea of 'spanner' in English as *llave* can in their own language. Students should be encouraged to check, where possible, before using a 'true' friend in a new context.
- *Are they used in the same styles?* Many cognates 'mean' the same but are used in different 'social' ways. For instance, *descend* in English 'means' the same as the French 'descendre', but it is used less frequently and in more literary styles.
- *Do they have the same grammar?* Two words may be very similar in meaning and use, but have different 'grammars'. For example, the Catalan word *sopar* is similar to 'supper' (as in *dinner*). But *sopar* is both a noun and a verb whereas English has no verb 'to supper'.

Some translation activities for the classroom

Correcting wrong translations

The teacher prepares some incorrect word for word translations and the students discuss them and correct them. This can be done with common phrases for example,

Spanish	¿Qué hora es?	¿Tiene fuego?
English	What hour is it? (i.e. What time is it?)	Have you fire? (i.e. Have you got a light?)

Or, at higher levels, the activity can focus on a specific aspect of grammar, for example, tense and time:

Spanish	Hace 2 años que vivo aquí.
English	I live here since 2 years. It's 2 years that I am living here. (i.e. I've been living here for 2 years.)

This sort of activity gets students to focus intensively on problematic areas and helps to make clear the dangers of word for word translation. Even though the focus is on individual phrases, it is a good idea to contextualise the practice through some sort of situation. This can often be done by using an 'L1 character' (e.g. 'Señor

Rodríguez' etc.) in an 'L2 situation, for example, Señor Rodríguez at the post office in England.

Consolidation translations

This kind of exercise gives the learners further practice in an area of grammar or vocabulary or a function which they've been studying recently.

The teacher writes a text in the L1 whose translation into English includes a number of examples of one particular area of difficulty. It's important to try to produce a text which sounds as realistic as possible, despite the fact that one area is being focused on. Some possible areas are as follows:

Grammar	**Vocabulary**	**Functions**
articles *(the/a)*	clothes	apologising
tenses	transport	giving advice
word order	shopping	suggestions
comparatives and superlatives	false friends	giving directions

The exercise doesn't always need to focus on a 'continuous' text; a dialogue might often be appropriate. The learners can be asked to do the translation itself for homework, then in class they can compare and discuss their different versions.

This kind of translation is done most frequently from the L1 to English. Its purpose is to give learners practice in *producing* a particular area of English, not just in understanding it.

> ACTIVITY
>
> Write an L1 text for translation, designed to practise one of the areas in the lists above. Make sure you include suitable information about context.

Comparing different versions (given by the teacher)

Consider the following example:

> Here is a letter from a bank manager to a customer, which you have been asked to translate. Read the letter, then look at the three translations of it. Discuss in groups which is the best translation.

23/7/92

Dear Mr Styles,

I regret to inform you that your account is again overdrawn, on this occasion by £227.

I would be grateful if you could contact me immediately to discuss the situation or failing this to take steps to remedy the situation as soon as possible.

I look forward to hearing from you.

Yours sincerely,

P.T. Williams
Manager

The students are then given three different translations of the text. The teacher can design the three translations so that each of them has different strengths and weaknesses. In this way, the students can discuss different aspects of this kind of letter, such as how to translate *Dear*, *Yours sincerely* and problematic expressions like *look forward to*. Finally, they can be asked to write in pairs or groups a new 'ideal' translation.

An activity like this should encourage students to think about aspects of context and to pay attention to the 'social' meaning of the words and phrases which they choose. In this particular case it also helps them to develop their ability to write formal letters in English. At lower levels much or all of the discussion may have to be done in the L1, but with more advanced learners it can involve them in a lot of useful listening and speaking practice too.

This activity can be done either from English to the L1 or the other way round. Obviously, any kind of text, not just letters, can be used in this way.

Comparing different versions (written by the students)

This is an intensive translation activity which works in the following way.

1. The teacher prepares two short texts for translation from English into the L1: text A and text B.
2. The students work in pairs. In each pair, one student gets text A and the other text B. They *don't* show each other their texts.
3. Individually, each student writes a quick translation of their text into the L1.
4. In each pair, the students exchange the translations that they've written. They *don't* give each other the original texts A and B.
5. Individually, each student writes a quick translation of the L1 text, which they now have, into the L2.

   At this point each student has translated *into* English the text that their partner translated *from* English.
6. In each pair, the students now show each other the original texts A and B. They compare their translations and discuss the differences between the two English versions of each text.

This activity is a good way of helping students to develop their awareness of the skills of translation and the differences between their own language and English. As in the case of the previous activity, the discussion (part 6) may have to take place in the L1.

Summary translation

There's no reason why activities should always involve translating *everything*. 'Real life' translation is often a question of giving an approximate version of the main ideas, and this can be done in the classroom too. For example, students can be asked to read an English text (perhaps from their coursebook) at home and prepare a rough oral translation of it. In class, different students take turns, paragraph by paragraph, in giving their L1 translations. This can be done at a brisk pace with any problems being cleared up on the spot – it doesn't have to be a lengthy activity. The idea is that most of the real work is done at home, so as to make the use of class time as efficient as possible.

Alternatively, the same can be done with a listening or reading exercise in class. The summary can be done in addition to or instead of 'standard' comprehension activities such as questions, true/false exercises etc.

Classroom interpreting

The teacher writes a dialogue between a speaker of the students' L1 and a native speaker of English; for example an English shopkeeper and, say, a Japanese visitor. The students are told that they need to act as interpreters while the shopkeeper speaks in English and the visitor in Japanese. The teacher plays the dialogue on a tape (or reads it) and either stops it after each sentence or plays it right through to the end while the students make notes. In either case, the students act as interpreters 'in both directions' (L1 – English and English – L1), which gives them useful and realistic practice.

These are only a small number of the ways in which teachers of monolingual classes can make use of translation as a stimulating, valuable activity. The next two chapters concentrate on ways in which teachers can help students in monolingual classes to make as much progress as possible.

Questions and further activities

1 Did translation play a part in your classes when you were learning English (or another language)? If so, was it helpful and interesting? Why (not)?
2 Decide which aspects of context it would be necessary to know about in order to translate the following sentence into your own language (or another language, if your own language is English): *I'm very sorry to hear about that.*
3 Design a 'comparing versions' activity and use it with one of your classes.

Reference

Translation by Alan Duff (Oxford 1989)

6 Making progress in the classroom

In most monolingual situations learners don't have very many English lessons, often as few as three or even two per week. In such circumstances the question of progress is particularly important, because the students' rate of progress can be quite slow – sometimes much slower than they and the teacher would like.

Progress in the classroom is obviously a very large topic. In this chapter, we're going to look briefly at four aspects of it which are especially significant for many teachers of monolingual classes:

- Learner training
- Setting and achieving realistic aims
- Motivation and class control
- Dealing with discipline problems.

Learner training

Learner training is about learning to learn. It involves getting students to think about *how* they learn and helping them to develop ways of learning as efficiently as possible.

Learner training can be relevant to any teaching situation but it's especially useful in monolingual classes, for two reasons:

1. The learners share a common culture. This means that training can focus on getting students to think about the sort of learning strategies and teachers' and learners' roles which are considered 'normal' in their own culture. Students can discuss with the teacher how appropriate their culture's 'traditional' approaches are for the learning of English.
2. The learners share a common language. Where possible, learner training should certainly take place in English, because this can give the learners valuable communicative practice. However, in many cases the learners' level or other factors will make the L1 the most appropriate language for some activities.

What are good learning strategies?

Here's an activity designed to make you think about some of your own beliefs and assumptions about learning strategies.

Look at the following statements about learning and communicating in English. Put a √ beside those which, in your opinion, represent the use of good strategies.

☐	A 'The teacher can't learn the language for me. The more I practise outside the classroom, the better.'	B 'I only say something in English if I'm absolutely sure it's correct.'	☐
☐	C 'I have to understand every word when I read something; otherwise there's no point in reading it.'	D 'I learn a lot of vocabulary by memorising lists of words with their equivalents in my own language.'	☐
☐	E 'I don't know anything about grammar and I don't want to. I just want to learn English.'	F 'I often practise on my own by making up conversations in my head.'	☐

A Students who realise the truth of this statement are in a good position to make further progress. Their desire for independence should be encouraged.

B Correctness is clearly very important. But this student needs to understand that nobody can be correct all the time. And, making mistakes and learning from them is also a way of learning to make fewer mistakes.

C Intensive, detailed work on reading texts can be very useful. But people read things all the time without understanding everything, in foreign languages and in their own language (see the section on reading in the next chapter).

D Why not? As long as the student is aware that there aren't always exact translation equivalents. And, of course, he or she needs to remember that learning vocabulary is not the same as practising *using* it.

E If some students find grammatical terminology difficult and confusing and want to avoid it where possible, then that's fine. But the teacher might want to show them that sometimes knowing about grammar can be a very useful short-cut in learning.

F Again, why not? This is a useful, personal strategy which many learners enjoy and find helpful.

We all have different ways of learning and teachers need to be careful about being too critical of any of their learners' strategies. But in some cases we need at least to encourage students to think about and perhaps adapt some of their strategies. And, of course, before doing any learner training with students, teachers need to think carefully about what their own views are. *How* learners learn is just as important as *what* they learn or how teachers teach.

Learner training in the classroom

Below are some examples of different types of learner training activities. As you consider them, decide whether it would be most appropriate for your students to do them in English or the L1, and why.

Questionnaires

Below is an example of a 'learner training questionnaire'.

Learning Questionnaire – February 9th

We're now halfway through the course. Please fill in this questionnaire at home and we'll discuss it during the next class.

In the course so far, have we had enough, too much or not enough of each of the following? Put a ✓ in the appropriate column.

	enough	too much	not enough
grammar work			
vocabulary work			
pronunciation work			
listening practice			
silent reading			
reading aloud			
discussions			
games			
role plays			
writing			
homework			

In the next class, the teacher discusses the results of the questionnaire with the learners. This can serve two purposes:

1 It gives the teacher feedback about how the learners feel about the course and allows him or her to change some aspects of the classes, where appropriate. This shows the learners that the teacher cares about their learning and respects their opinions.

   For example, most of the learners might feel that they're being given too much homework. If they can convince the teacher that they're really finding it difficult to do as much as they're receiving, the teacher might agree to give them a little less for a while.
2 It provides a good opportunity to do some learner training as such. It may show the teacher that the group are confused about some aspects of how to learn best. Let's say, for instance, that the teacher believes that doing a lot of reading aloud in class isn't very useful, but the questionnaire results may show that the students feel that they're not doing *enough* reading aloud. If so, this is an opportunity for the teacher to discuss this technique with the learners and explain to them the reservations that he or she has about it. In this way, the learners may develop a better understanding of the relationship between silent reading and reading aloud and the best ways of developing reading skills.

Training exercises

The teacher may decide to use some activities to encourage the learners to think more about a specific aspect of their learning. Over the page you will find an example also connected with reading.

Example 1

2 Reading strategies

A good reader varies his or her reading strategy according to *why* he or she is reading. Having a reason for reading helps you to focus on what you need or want to understand.

When might you use the following strategies?
a) *Skimming:* reading a text quickly just to understand the main ideas.
b) *Scanning:* having a specific point in mind and looking for it quickly in a text.
c) *Reading for detail:* reading a whole text very carefully for specific information.

Can you think of a situation where you really need to understand every word of what you are reading? Give an example if you can.

Activity: Reading a menu

What strategy would you use to read this menu? Why?

Browns Restaurant & Bar

SPAGHETTI
All spaghetti orders served with Garlic Bread and Mixed Salad with a choice of Blue Cheese, Thousand Island, French Dressing, Mayonnaise, Garlic Dressing
ITALIAN TOMATO SAUCE onion, peppers, tomato and red wine £4.35
TRADITIONAL MEAT SAUCE prime mince, herbs and more £4.35
BRIGHTON SEAFOOD SAUCE mussels, prawns and more £4.35
CHEF'S SPECIAL SAUCE ask your waitress £4.65
ANY COMBINATION OF TWO OF THE ABOVE SAUCES £4.65
A PORTION FOR CHILDREN without a salad and garlic bread £2.85

SALADS
With a choice of Blue Cheese,
Thousand Island, French Dressing, Mayonnaise, Garlic Dressing
MRS BROWNS VEGETARIAN £4.95
TUNA FISH SALAD £5.65
CRAB AND AVOCADO SALAD £4.95
AVOCADO, BACON AND SPINACH SALAD £5.45
HOT CHICKEN SALAD with fresh herbs and greens £4.95
CAESAR SALAD iceberg, parmesan, anchovies, croutons with garlic dressing £4.95
HOT FILLET SALAD pan-fried strips of beef with spices £6.15

MEAT FISH AND SPECIAL
All dishes served with Fried or Baked Potato (with butter or sour cream) and Vegetable of the Day or Mixed Salad, with a choice of Blue Cheese, Thousand Island, French Dressing, Mayonnaise, Garlic Dressing
SCOTCH SIRLOIN STEAK half pound, with herb butter £7.35
BROWNS LEG OF LAMB chargrilled with rosemary, served with Oxford Sauce £7.15
FRESH FISH IN SEASON £6.55
PRIME ROAST RIBS with barbecue sauce £5.65
PEASANTS POT pork, chilli, butter beans, red wine and more £4.95
FISHERMANS PIE with cheddar cheese crust £4.85
STEAK MUSHROOM AND GUINNESS PIE £4.95
COUNTRY CHICKEN PIE £4.85
CHARGRILLED TURKEY BREAST £5.45
FRESH VEGETABLES IN A GREEN HERB SAUCE £4.85

DAILY CHEF'S SPECIALS on the BLACKBOARD

SIDE ORDERS
Mixed Salad £1.05   Garlic Bread per Person 75p
Fried Potatoes £1.05   Fresh Vegetable of the Day £1.05
Fresh Mushrooms £1.35

SANDWICHES

A good reader uses the layout of a text to help him or her understand it. What features of layout helped you to read the menu?

Projects

Learner training activities can be used as a regular part of a whole course and the teacher can design a 'learner training syllabus'. Students can be asked to keep a special folder or exercise book for this part of their course. Below are two examples of introductions to this kind of course, one in English only and the other in the L1 and English.

Example 2

---

1 WEEK INTENSIVE COURSE

Level: Lower-intermediate
Hours: 30

Aim: This course aims to help you develop your knowledge of the English language in general, to improve your understanding of natural spoken English and to increase your confidence and fluency in speaking the language. The course will introduce you to a variety of ways of learning and practising English and help you to develop your own strategies for continuing to learn after the course.

Content: As well as activities which are designed to improve your understanding of spoken English and your fluency, your grammatical problems will be diagnosed and covered in special sessions. There will also be special sessions of 'learner training', which aim to help you discover ways of learning English which are best for you. For example, you will have a look at how to increase your vocabulary.

Activities: The course will include activities where you work in pairs or groups with other students, listening to cassettes, watching videos, using the computers, role play, games and making a video film, etc. A qualified and experienced teacher whose mother tongue is English will be with you at all times to help, advise and teach you.

```
                PROJECT 1987

            LEARNING TO LEARN ENGLISH

A chacun sa façon d'apprendre. Notre objectif
est de vous aider à découvrir personnellement
le meilleur moyen d'apprendre l'anglais.
Apprendre à apprendre c'est ce que nous
appelons le 'learner training'.

Vous utiliserez ce dossier avec votre manuel
d'anglais. En classe vous échangerez avec vos
camarades vos idées sur l'apprentissage des
langues étrangères afin de partager vos
différentes expériences.


(Everybody learns in a different way. Our aim is to
help you discover the best way for you to learn
English. Learning how to learn is called 'learner
training'.
  You will use this project with your English
coursebook. In class you will discuss your ideas
about learning foreign languages with the other
pupils so that you may learn from each other.)
```

Interviews

In some situations, teachers occasionally have opportunities for individual tutorials with learners to discuss their progress. It can be very helpful to use opportunities of this kind to discuss not just *how much* progress students are making, but also aspects of *how they're learning*, both in class and outside. The teacher may be able to give students advice about strategies which will help them to improve more quickly.

The role of the L1 in learner training

What did you decide about each of the above activities, as regards the language in which it would be best to do it? It seems to me that there are two main reasons for doing learner training in the L1:

- If the learners don't have enough English to do the activity *in* English.
- If the learners *need* training in the L1.

For instance, the reading comprehension activity opposite involves the important skill of *guessing meaning from context*. Some learners find this sort of skill very difficult to develop. In such cases, it can be a good idea to do some learner training in the L1 first. For example, in the case of example 3 the teacher could give the students an L1 reading comprehension exercise and then discuss with them how they were able to do it. After that, the class moves on to an exercise in English.

The same technique can help with the development of many other skills, such as skimming a text for general information, scanning for specific information, writing 'coherent' texts, writing summaries, etc. – in effect, any skill which may cause difficulties in the L1. It's important to bear in mind, however, that sometimes skills can be learned *through* English, even if the learners don't have them in the L1.

Note: It isn't possible in this book to look at all the different types of learner training activities that teachers can use. *Learning to Learn English* by Gail Ellis and Barbara Sinclair is a very useful course in learner training which includes a teacher's book and a cassette.

Example 3

The Loneliness of the Long-Distance Runner

On I went, out of the wood, passing the man leading without knowing I was going to do so. Flip-flap, flip-flap, jog-trot, jog-trot, crunchslap-crunchslap, across the middle of the broad field again, rythmically running in my greyhound effortless fashion, knowing I had run the race though it wasn't half over, knowing I could win if I wanted to, could go on for ten or fifteen or twenty miles if I had to and drop dead at the finish of it. But I'm not going to win because winning means running straight into their white-gloved hands and grinning mugs, and staying there for the rest of my natural long life.

Glossary
greyhound a fast racing dog
mug (coll) face

VOCABULARY

1 Find words or expressions in the extract which mean:

1 going ahead of somebody in a race
2 without needing to try hard
3 continue
4 smiling broadly

> ACTIVITY
>
> A What sort of learner strategies are typical in your learners' culture? Make a list of these, e.g:
>
> - The learners prefer to listen to the teacher rather than speak themselves.
> - They always want to write down new words as soon as they're introduced in class.
> - They expect to receive a lot of homework.
>
> B Which of these 'typical' strategies indicate a need for some learner training activities? Which kinds of activities would be most appropriate in your situation? Prepare some activities and try them out with one of your classes.

Setting and achieving realistic aims

In most monolingual classes learners can only devote a relatively small amount of time to English per week and they spend at least several years studying the language. In these circumstances it's essential for the teacher to establish clear and appropriate learning objectives. Students need to know how much they can hope to achieve and how much they're expected to achieve by the end of a particular year or course. One procedure for doing this is:

Set aims

Decide what you can realistically hope to achieve in a particular term or semester. This may be dictated for you by the syllabus in a coursebook e.g. 'finish book 1 by the end of year 1' or something like that. If so, then you need to decide whether or not it's possible to cover everything in the syllabus in the time allowed – your own and other colleagues' experience will be very valuable here. Does the syllabus provide enough work for the year? Is there anything you feel should be added? What should be left out? If you leave things out, will this be a problem at exam time? All of these questions need to be considered and, if possible, discussed.

Tell the students what your aims are

Students should know, from the beginning of a course, where they're expected to get to and when. However, many syllabuses are written in purely grammatical terms, i.e. they only give lists of grammatical structures which are covered in the book. In this case, it's useful to make clear to students some of the things which they'll learn to *do* with English as well. For example, *introducing oneself*, *making a simple phone call*, and so on. This is less 'dry' than pure grammar and it helps to remind learners that 'doing the *present simple*' or 'doing prepositions' isn't enough – they have to be able to do things *with* their knowledge. At lower levels, teachers may need to discuss this with the students in the L1.

Build in flexibility

All sorts of factors will influence how easy or difficult it is for teachers to achieve the aims which they've set – the students' ability and motivation, events outside the classroom, etc. On the other hand, once aims have been set, they should, as a general rule, be achieved. If, in our example, book 1 isn't finished by the end of year 1, this may well cause problems in year 2 and it is likely to have a negative effect on the learners' motivation and confidence in the teacher. In order to finish a syllabus by a certain time, therefore, it's often necessary to be flexible about such things as the amount of controlled practice in the classroom, the number of communicative activities, the amount of 'recycling' of language, the number of writing activities done in class, how much homework the students do, and so on. Adjustments can be made throughout the course to make sure that the class is always 'on target' as regards the syllabus.

Review aims regularly and adjust them where necessary

If aims can't be achieved without consistently sacrificing important types of classroom activities (e.g. proper practice, communicative activities etc.), then the aims need to be changed. There's no point in racing through a syllabus which is too long just to get to the end of it – even if the students have 'finished book 1', they won't have *learned* very much. Syllabuses decided by a school, an exam board or a government ministry may, of course, be very difficult to change. If so, then in the meantime it's a question of being as flexible as possible and making careful decisions about how the students can learn as much as possible while still using the current syllabus.

> ACTIVITY
>
> If you don't use a procedure of this kind already, try it out at the beginning of your next term or course. If possible, discuss things with colleagues who use the same syllabuses as yourself. Work together on finding ways of making your aims as realistic as possible by building sufficient flexibility into your teaching.

In any teaching situation, there will always be some factors which the teacher can't change (e.g. size of classes, number of lessons per week etc.) – the teacher's job is to help the students to make as much progress as possible *in the circumstances*. All teachers have a responsibility to make sure that their students are as successful as possible, allowing for the time and resources available. No teacher can do more than that.

Motivation and class control

Motivation is one of the most important factors in any language learning situation. After all, if learners are highly motivated, they'll learn *something* in even the most difficult situation. And if they *aren't* motivated, they probably won't learn much, even with lots of class time, small classes and excellent resources.

Some learners have 'guaranteed' motivation right from the start. Often this is either because they have very positive feelings about some aspects of the 'target' culture (e.g. American rock music or English literature etc.) or because they hope to get a job which involves using English (e.g. *I want to be a pilot with our national airline and I'll need English for that*). Unfortunately, in monolingual classes such learners are frequently in a minority. The majority don't *have* a specific goal in learning English. For these learners, whether they feel motivated and enthusiastic about learning English will depend on many factors. Two of these are:

- their relationship with the teacher and with each other
- the sort of lessons which the teacher gives.

If the relationships in the classroom are of mutual trust and respect and if the classes are stimulating and enjoyable, then motivation is likely to be high. We'll look at each of these two areas in more detail in a moment.

Many teachers of monolingual classes work mainly with children and adolescents. There's no doubt that for many teachers and young learners, one of the most important factors in their work is class control. Motivated students generally behave well, so helping to create and maintain a high level of enthusiasm should be one of the teacher's first priorities:

> The more you can do about motivation, the less you'll need to worry about classroom control.

Relationships in the classroom

The appropriate sort of relationships in any classroom depend on the culture in which the classes are taking place. However, there are some principles which apply in most circumstances:

> **Classroom relationships: 7 general principles**
> 1 Make sure students know the rules.
> 2 Appear confident.
> 3 Learn the students' names.
> 4 Make sure students listen to each other.
> 5 Make sure students know why they're doing an activity.
> 6 Be flexible.
> 7 Be realistic about the L1 in the classroom.

The Rules

It's very important that a group should know from the beginning what is and what isn't acceptable behaviour. In some situations it's possible to 'negotiate' the rules with a group; the students then feel that they have been involved in creating the rules and are therefore more likely to obey them. And, if necessary, part or all of this negotiation can be done in the L1.

In a typical class, rules will probably deal with points such as:

- not bringing books and materials to class
- not doing homework
- lateness
- using the L1 at inappropriate times

- talking at the wrong time
- not paying attention
- eating or drinking in class
- cheating in tests.

It should be clear to the students what will happen if rules are broken and the teacher should be consistent about this.

Confidence

Nobody is completely confident! All of us have worries and doubts about aspects of our teaching, particularly in the first months and years in the classroom. However, being confident is not the same thing as *appearing* confident.

It is sometimes useful to 'force' a confidence that you don't necessarily feel. The more confident a teacher appears, the more confidence the students will have in him or her. And 'forcing' oneself to appear confident can often help one to develop greater *genuine* confidence!

Names

> *What do you think the answer to number 3 is, Patricia?*

Learning and using the names of the students in a group as quickly as possible is very important. It encourages the development of a good working relationship, it is useful from the point of view of efficient class management and it can be helpful when dealing with discipline problems. A teacher who can intervene in an activity by saying, for example, *Claudia, you seem to be talking a lot of Italian* rather than, *You, no you to the left ... yes, you ...* to an anonymous pupil, is likely to have much more influence.

Note: Mary Underwood's book in this series *Effective Class Management* suggests a number of techniques for learning and remembering students' names.

Listening to each other

If each student is expected to listen to what other class members say, rather than just concentrating on his or her own contribution, then this will help to create a disciplined environment in which learning can take place. Activities which require co-operation, sharing of ideas, reaching an agreement etc. can help to encourage this.

The purpose of activities

Most students are more willing to do certain activities if they understand exactly how those activities are supposed to help their learning. This is where learner training comes in!

Flexibility

Although it's important to maintain consistent 'rules' of behaviour in the classroom, it's also true that teachers need to be flexible about when to do what. A grammar presentation may be right for one time and a game for another. The decision will depend on all kinds of factors which may include the stage of the term, the day of the week, the time of day, etc. If a particular activity really isn't working, perhaps because the students are finding it difficult to concentrate due to an approaching outside event such as a holiday, then it's sometimes best to 'give in' discreetly and do something less demanding. On the other hand, it can be dangerous to allow students to believe that they can get out of doing 'hard work' whenever they feel like it. The ideal is a teacher who is seen to mix firmness and flexibility.

The L1/L2 balance

As we've said before, the teacher should aim for as much L2 as possible in the classroom. But L1 problem clinics, breaks to 'let off steam' in the L1 and so on all have their place. And even the occasional bit of inappropriate L1 use isn't the end of the world!

The lessons themselves

What takes place in lessons is obviously just as important as the relationship which the teacher has with the students. Three crucial points in this respect are the following:

Participation

Students need practice, especially in monolingual classes where they don't have many hours per week or many opportunities to practise outside the classroom. Lessons which consist of lectures about English by the teacher usually produce bored students who don't make much progress. It's the students who are learning the language so in general it's them who should do most of the talking. 'Interactive' teacher-led activities and plenty of pair and group work will help to ensure that this is the case.

Success

We've already looked at the importance of realistic aims. Learners need to be challenged, but they also need to be *successful,* at least some of the time. It isn't always easy to get this right, especially in mixed level classes. But as teachers, we need to keep trying to use activities which allow most learners to be successful most of the time. A sense of achievement is a fundamental aspect of motivation which all learners should be allowed to experience.

Note: There is a clear link between success and the area of error and correction. *Mistakes and Correction* by Julian Edge in this series has a lot to say about this.

Variety

People tend to get bored with anything which is always done in exactly the same way. All classes, particularly with younger learners, should include a variety of different types of activities. This is partly for reasons of motivation and partly to make sure that learners get practice in all the different kinds of skills which learning a language involves.

Using a good variety of classroom activities obviously involves preparing lessons properly. If your time is limited, it's important to remember that a little preparation can go a long way. With experience and practice it's possible to prepare stimulating classes quite quickly. A little preparation is far better than none at all. Of course, students usually know when a teacher is unprepared and this inevitably affects the working relationship they have.

ACTIVITY

Design a series of six lessons for one of your own classes, including a suitable variety of activities. Make sure that there's a balance of new language and revision, 'difficult' and 'easy' activities and different language skills (e.g. speaking, listening, etc.).

Dealing with discipline problems

Motivation is the key to avoiding discipline problems and 'prevention' is certainly better than 'cure'. But the teacher of younger learners who never has to deal with any problems of this sort is a lucky exception. Sometimes things *do* go wrong.

In most situations of indiscipline or bad behaviour the following principles are crucial:

> Apply the rules.
>
> Don't lose the learners' respect / maintain a good relationship with them.
>
> Explore the causes of the problems.

Applying the rules

We've already mentioned the importance of establishing a set of rules for classroom behaviour. But it's only worth doing this if when a rule is broken, the teacher *does* something about it.

Rules which the learners aren't expected to obey are almost as bad as having no rules at all. It's up to the teacher to decide exactly *what* to do. He or she might decide, for instance, to:

- put things right with a significant 'look'
- say something to the student(s)
- give a punishment of some kind
- speak to the student(s) after the class.

A teacher might also decide, if the problem is a persistent one, to reconsider the rule in question. Perhaps it needs changing or even abandoning, if not with the present group then with a future one.

In some cases it may well be necessary to use the L1 in dealing with discipline problems, for example when speaking to a student individually after a class. However, it's important not to fall into the trap of using the L1 *routinely* to do things which could reasonably be done in English. Phrases like *Stop talking now, Dimitrios* or *Are you listening, Stephanie?* can be understood by students of *any* level (even if the teacher needs to use gesture, facial expression, mime etc. as well).

Maintaining a good relationship

In general, learners respect teachers who respect *them* and set an example. So:

Do be fair and avoid having favourites or 'victimising' students.
Do be consistent.
Do carry out threats (if you make them).
Do punish the action, not the person.
Don't get angry or lose control of yourself.

Don't shout.
Don't ridicule or make fun of students.
Don't bear grudges.

It isn't always easy to keep one's temper or to avoid shouting etc. But the ideal to aim for in most circumstances is a calm teacher who means what he or she says and maintains control, while continuing to respect the learners as *people*. Adolescents, in particular, are very sensitive to adults' opinions of them. If discipline problems are dealt with in ways which they see as a personal attack on them, this is likely to cause resentment and make the problems worse. On the other hand, learners need to feel that the teacher is the ultimate authority in the classroom. If this isn't clear, it tends to lead to insecurity and, in its own way, discipline problems. A culturally acceptable relationship of mutual respect is usually the best solution.

Exploring causes of problems

If a student is persistently badly behaved, there are always reasons for this. And very frequently they're more than just 'I don't like English'. Progress can sometimes be made by finding out from other teachers, parents, the student etc. if there are emotional or learning difficulties or circumstances at home which are affecting the student's behaviour. On the other hand, if a whole group are regularly difficult to control and motivate, there may be aspects of your teaching which they don't understand or react negatively to. In this case, some negotiation and learner training may be necessary.

If necessary, how can the school help me?

Finally, in extreme cases, teachers should know what sort of help they can get from the institution and at what point this is available. If this isn't clear in your own situation, it may be worth getting together with other teachers and asking the school to develop a clear policy.

In this chapter we've discussed a number of ways of helping students to make progress in the classroom. The next chapter deals with the question of progress outside the classroom.

Questions and further activities

1 Do most of your own students need to be motivated by the classes themselves? Or do they have very clear reasons for

learning English? If so, in what ways can you make your classes 'fit' the students' reasons for learning?

2 Design a set of rules for your classroom. Which is better, to announce them or negotiate them with the students? Suggest reasons for your answer. If you decide to negotiate them, it's usually much better to do this with new groups rather than students that you already teach. If you need to do it with students that you have already, try to do so at the beginning of a new year or term.

3 What *exactly* would you do in the following situations? Would you use the L1 at all? You may feel that in some cases you need more information before deciding. If so, *what* information do you need? (*In all cases, the students are elementary level.*)

   A Whenever you ask student A to say something in English, you can't hear her reply. You've asked her several times to speak more loudly, but she doesn't.
   B Student B is regularly late for class. You've tried to find out if he has a problem, but he just says he can't help it.
   C Student C seems to enjoy pair and group work activities, but she always ends up speaking more of the L1 than English!

4 Make a list of the areas in which your learners most need learner training. Design some activities to help them. (Refer to *Learning to Learn English* if possible.)

References

1 *Learning to Learn English* by Gail Ellis and Barbara Sinclair (Cambridge 1989)
2 *Effective Classroom Management* by Mary Underwood (Longman 1987)
3 *Mistakes and Correction* by Julian Edge (Longman 1989)
4 *Example 1* from *Learning to Learn English Student's Book* by Gail Ellis and Barbara Sinclair (Cambridge 1989)
5 *Example 2* from *Learning to Learn English Teacher's Book* by Gail Ellis and Barbara Sinclair (Cambridge 1989)
6 *Example 3* from *Blueprint Intermediate* by Brian Abbs and Ingrid Freebairn (Longman 1989)

7 Making progress outside the classroom

Progress in the classroom is vital, but in most monolingual situations it's limited by the low number of class hours which students have. For this reason, any learning which can take place in the students' own time is extremely important too, particularly since it allows individual learners to work at their own pace and use the learning styles which suit them best.

However, while learning outside the classroom can be relatively easy in multilingual situations in English-speaking countries, it's not such a simple matter in most monolingual contexts. Teachers and students need to be aware of the opportunities for 'open learning' (learning without a teacher present) which exist in their particular situation. Below is a list of the main ways in which students in non-English-speaking situations can learn and practise outside class time. Read the list and put a √ by each of the ways which you encourage your students to use already.

- doing homework ☐
- reading magazines written for learners of English ☐
- watching TV or videos, going to the cinema ☐
- writing to pen friends ☐
- reading books, comics, newspapers ☐
- listening to the radio, cassettes, records ☐
- using self-access centres ☐
- talking to local native speakers of English ☐

We'll now look at each of these ways in more detail.

Homework

The main advantage of homework is that all the learners do an activity in their own time and at their own speed, *in addition* to everything that they do in the classroom.

The big problem, of course, is time: the students' time and the teacher's time. It is important in monolingual situations to try and keep the rhythm going between classes. If a group has no English lessons from Thursday to Tuesday then something they may seem to have learned well one day may be completely forgotten by the next lesson. For this reason:

> Students should do something at home after every lesson even if it only takes 5 or 10 minutes.
>
> Teachers shouldn't have to spend too much time marking. Preparing lessons as well as possible is vital, and marking shouldn't interfere with this.

Homework does not have to involve writing something and handing it in for the teacher to mark. There are all sorts of useful types of homework:

Preparing an exercise

Example 1

> HOMEWORK
>
> *Re-arrange the sentences to make a question.*
>
> (1) Where he live does?
> (2) Smith Mr where does work?
> (3) When get up does he?
> (4) What do does he?

At the beginning of the next class, the teacher checks that all the students have done the exercise(s) and then elicits the correct answers. The teacher won't always know which students have done well or badly. The main thing is that every student has done the exercise and finds out whether he or she has got it right or wrong.

Learning vocabulary

Example 2

> *Insert the correct word in the gaps below.*
> (1) He asked for a t........ to London.
> (2) The bus conductor asked him for his f........ .
> (3) He waited at the b........ s........ for ten minutes.
> (4) The car ran out of p........ so they had to go to a g........ .
> (5) The plane didn't leave the a........ on time as it was d........ by fog.

During the next class, the teacher checks quickly whether the students have filled the gaps correctly.

Reading

The teacher asks the students to read a chapter of a story in their coursebook or a class reader. The students can be asked either to do a task included in the coursebook, or one set by the teacher.

Preparing for a speaking activity

Students prepare to take part in a role play or a discussion, either from the coursebook or set by the teacher.

Preparing for an L1 problem clinic

The class are asked to revise some chapters in the coursebook and prepare questions for the next lesson.

If the resources are available and the students are of the right level, there's no reason why homework shouldn't involve, for example, watching TV or listening to the radio in English, using a dictionary workbook (see chapter 8) or using a self-access centre (see further on in the chapter). What you can do depends very much on your own circumstances – but it is always worth looking for ways of giving students something more than 'traditional' homework activities.

A final word about homework

When homework *is* handed in, it must be marked and it must be marked reasonably quickly and thoroughly. A teacher who forgets about a pile of compositions, or returns them a month later, or doesn't mark them properly isn't doing much for the students' motivation. This is another reason for not getting students to hand in too much written homework.

ACTIVITY

Do you give your classes some homework after each lesson? If not, try doing so as an experiment. After a few weeks, review the situation and discuss it with the students.

Reading

Most coursebooks have reading texts and exercises in them. These are helpful, but usually they aren't enough. Students need practice in reading longer texts too, and they need practice in *reading for pleasure*. If you can get your students to read in English for pleasure regularly, this can help their progress enormously:

- Reading for pleasure is learning English.
- Reading for pleasure is learning to read better in English.
- Reading for pleasure gives students confidence and helps to maintain motivation.
- Reading for pleasure helps learners to become independent of the teacher.

What should students read?

And, in many ways, *it doesn't matter what they read*. It can be a specially designed 'reader', a book written for native speakers, a magazine or a comic. The important thing is that the students should be interested in what they read and enjoy it. When this happens, they usually concentrate on the ideas in the text more than the language itself. At the same time they see again structures and vocabulary which they have already studied and they read and understand new language items too.

It is important for students to be aware that *they don't need to understand every word*. If they can understand enough to read with enjoyment, that's enough! After all, when they read for pleasure in their own language they don't understand every word, so why should they expect to understand everything in a foreign language?

Note: Most major ELT publishers now produce a series of readers for students at various levels. In addition to this, Mary Glasgow publish a number of magazines for learners. Their address is given on page 91. 'Dual' texts written in both English and the L1 are also available from some publishers.

Listening and watching

The same points that we made about reading apply here – listening and watching for pleasure are just as important as reading for pleasure, whether it is material intended for native speakers or material produced specifically for learners of English.

Materials for native speakers

Sources of material include local radio or TV programmes in English, cinema films (including subtitled versions), songs on cassettes or records, hired or bought video cassettes, etc.

Much of this material will be very challenging for learners and the teacher will need to emphasise the importance of understanding the main ideas rather than all the details. If learners feel that they're understanding enough (however little this may be) in order to enjoy a song, a programme or a film, then they should be encouraged to continue. Learners may wish to see a film in the L1 before watching it in English, or to listen to the day's news on an L1 radio station and then tune to an English language station to listen again. This should be encouraged. Subtitles too can make otherwise 'impossible' films accessible. They provide learners with rich opportunities to compare how all kinds of concepts are expressed in the L1 and English.

For low level students the best option is short TV programmes which include a lot of visual help, for example cartoons or the weather forecast.

A note on songs

If you are using songs for classroom activities:

- Students should understand that listening to songs is especially difficult. Frequently, native speakers have to listen to a song several times before they feel that they really 'understand' it.

- There are often words in a song which are difficult to understand, *however* many times you listen to it. Sometimes songwriters use unusual vocabulary or the singing makes it difficult to distinguish all the words.
- It is quite possible to listen to and enjoy songs without understanding them 'completely' – we do it all the time! Frequently there isn't one 'correct' way of understanding a song; different people will interpret the same song in different ways.

Materials produced for learners of English

These have the advantage of being simpler and more accessible for lower level learners. Nevertheless, they should always be seen as a step on the road to using 'real' material. The main sources of materials of this kind are local radio and television programmes for learners of English, BBC World Service programmes (see page 91) and BBC English broadcasts (see also page 91). These offer a wide variety of learners' programmes for all levels and ages, simplified 'authentic' material, courses accompanied by books and cassettes, question and answer programmes about the English language, drama, 'soap operas', comedy and so on. BBC English also broadcasts programmes for *teachers* of English, on teaching methodology, language problems etc.

ACTIVITY

Make a list of the 'listening and watching' resources which your students can exploit. Make sure that they're aware of these and suggest ways in which they can use them.

Self-access centres

A self-access centre is a place where facilities are available for students to learn and practise outside class time. It might be anything from just a few sets of exercises with keys, to a centre which includes books, magazines, listening and recording booths, individual video machines and computers etc. The self-access area can be anything from a corner of a classroom available for limited periods of time every week, to a special room available whenever the institution is open.

Self-access centres allow teachers to suggest to individual learners that they do specific types of work on specific aspects of the language.

Note: *Self-access* by Susan Sheerin (Oxford 1989) is a thorough, practical guide to setting up, developing and using self-access centres. *Self-Instruction in Language Learning* by Leslie Dickinson (Cambridge 1987) is also very useful for teachers interested in open learning.

Speaking and writing

Writing to pen friends can be very good practice. It's a 'real' writing activity which many students find very motivating. Reading a pen friend's replies is good practice too. In the case of younger learners, it can also be of considerable educational value as regards finding out about other cultures and ways of life.

You may be able to help your students find pen friends through links that your school has with institutions in other countries. Otherwise, an international magazine where learners advertise for pen friends is *Practical English Teaching*, published by Mary Glasgow (address on page 91).

Finding opportunities to *speak* English outside the classroom can be difficult. Local events in English (talks, films, concerts, etc.) are often a good starting point for adult learners as regards meeting speakers of English. Often, these will be people who themselves are studying the learners' language. In this case, a common option is a 'conversation exchange' between two people: for an hour a week they speak English and for another hour they speak the learner's L1.

You can also encourage your students to:

- speak English to each other during breaks;
- practise with relatives or family friends who have a higher level of English than their own;
- make up dialogues or practise 'in their own heads' to fill in 'dead' times of the day – in the shower, on the bus, etc.

Questions and further activities

1 Do you have a class library or a self-access centre? Does your school have a library? Are suitable books in English available for students to read outside class time? If not, could any funds be made available to develop this kind of resource? If the school can't provide funds, are there any local institutions or businesses which might be able to help?
2 Should pen friends of learners of English always be native speakers of English? Are there any reasons why they shouldn't be other non-native speakers from different cultures?
3 What about 'conversation exchange' partners? Should they always be native speakers of English? Why (not)?
4 Are there any other types of 'real' writing activities which students can be encouraged to use outside the classroom? For example, in connection with class projects.

Useful addresses

- Mary Glasgow Publications Ltd., Brookhampton Lane, Kineton, Warwick CV35 0BR, Great Britain (publisher of *Practical English Teaching* and magazines for learners of English).
- 'London Calling', P. O. Box 76 S, The BBC, Bush House, The Strand, London WC2B 4PH, Great Britain (for a free schedule of World Service programmes).
- BBC English, P.O. Box 76, The BBC (same address as above).

References

1 *Self-access* by Susan Sheerin (Oxford 1989)
2 *Self-Instruction in Language Learning* by Leslie Dickinson (Cambridge 1987)

- Both examples in this chapter are originals.

8 'English only' and bilingual dictionaries

A dictionary is one of the oldest and most basic resources available to teachers and learners of a foreign language. Yet many teachers are very uncertain about different types of dictionaries and which are best for them and their students. 'English only' learner's dictionaries are very popular nowadays and teachers are sometimes told that these are 'better' than the more traditional bilingual type. But is this true? The purpose of this chapter is to look briefly at the main types of dictionaries now available and discuss their advantages and disadvantages.

> ACTIVITY
>
> Make a list of all the dictionaries (connected with English) which are available in your own situation, including:
> - dictionaries which you own;
> - dictionaries which your students own;
> - dictionaries which your school or college owns;
> - dictionaries available in your local library or other institutions where you live.

Keep the list, so that you can refer to it again later in the chapter.

'English only' learner's dictionaries

These are dictionaries which are written specifically for learners of English, entirely *in* English. They are normally designed to be used by learners from any L1 background. This kind of dictionary has a number of important advantages:

- The authors have learners in mind when they write the dictionary and they try to use the simplest possible definitions and to give as many examples of use as they can.

- Many dictionaries of this kind have 'user's guides' which help students to get as much as possible out of the dictionary. Example 1 is taken from the guide to the *Longman Dictionary of Contemporary English (LDOCE)*.

Example 1

---

2 Use your dictionary to help you find the missing prepositions and adverbs in these sentences:

1 We **waited** .... ten o'clock.

2 We couldn't **wait** .... him any longer.

3 He has a **diploma** .... accountancy.

4 Do fines **deter** people .... dropping litter in our streets and parks?

5 The words were all **jumbled** .... and the students had to **sort** them .... to form correct sentences.

6 Princess Margaret, Princess Anne and Princess Diana are all **related** .... Queen Elizabeth by birth or by marriage.

- There are always words which are difficult or impossible to translate from one language to another. Because this type of dictionary is written in English, explanations can be given of 'untranslatable' words.
- Learner's dictionaries in English often give a lot of additional information on important areas for students. *The Oxford Advanced Learner's Dictionary (OALD)* for example, includes a detailed guide to the different verb patterns of English and the *Longman Dictionary of Contemporary English (LDOCE)* uses a system of 'Language Notes' on particularly difficult aspects of grammar, style etc., as in Example 2 overleaf.
- Finally, as we have emphasised throughout this book, you can only learn English if you practise. Learner's dictionaries in English encourage students to understand English *through* English and to think *in* English.

Example 2

■ Language Note: Articles

■ Are you talking about things and people in general?

When nouns appear in general statements, they can be used with different articles, depending on whether they are countable or uncountable.

In general statements, countable nouns can be used

in the plural without an article:

> Elephants have tusks.|I like elephants.

in the singular with **the**:

> The elephant is a magnificent animal.|He is studying the elephant in its natural habitat.

in the singular with **a/an**:

> An elephant can live for a very long time.

Note that **a/an** can only be used in this way if the noun is the grammatical subject of the sentence.

In general statements, uncountable nouns are always used

without an article:

> Photography is a popular hobby.|She's interested in photography.|Water is essential to life.

Are 'English only' dictionaries really always the best solution?

These are some of the reasons why 'English only' dictionaries have become so popular. It is important to remember, however, that this kind of dictionary has definite limitations:

- Most learner's dictionaries in English aren't suitable for beginners and very elementary students. You obviously need a certain level of English to be able to understand even simple entries.
- *Circularity*. 'Circularity' means using word A to define word B and also using word B to define word A. For example:

If a dictionary uses the word 'illness' to define *disease* and then uses 'disease' to define *illness*, the problem is obvious – if the users of the dictionary don't know these words already, then the dictionary won't be of much help.

- *You can't look up words which you don't know!* You can use this kind of dictionary to find information about a word which you don't understand, can't use properly, or can't pronounce. But it is of no use to a learner who wants to know how to say 'x' or 'y' in English.

Bilingual dictionaries

These are dictionaries which give lists of words and translations in two languages.

Example 3

advice [əd·vais]*n* consejo *m*; (*report*) informe *m*, noticia *f*; **a piece of** — un consejo; **my** — **to you is** + *infin* te aconsejo + *infin*; **to ask for** —, **to seek** — pedir consejos; **to take someone's** — seguir los consejos de uno; **to take legal** — consultar a un abogado; **to take medical** — consultar a un médico.

Example 4

consejo *nm* (a) **un** — a piece of advice; a hint; **su** — his advice, his counsel; **agradezco el** — I am grateful for your advice; **pedir** — **a uno** to ask someone for advice, ask someone's advice; — **pericial** expert advice; —**s** advice. (b) (*Pol etc*) council; (*Comm*) board; (*Law*) tribunal; court; — **de administración** board of directors; —**de disciplina** disciplinary board; — **de ministros** cabinet; cabinet meeting; — **privado** privy council; — **de guerra** court-martial; — **de guerra sumarísimo** drumhead court-martial.

This is, for many people, the 'traditional' kind of dictionary for students of languages. Good modern dictionaries of this kind are extremely useful in that they combine translations with examples and relevant information about the grammar and use of words, as in. Here, the authors show that *advice* is uncountable by giving the plural 'consejos' as *advice*. They also help learners choose which word to use in a certain context.

Another significant strength of bilingual dictionaries is, of course, that absolute beginners can use them. Unlike the 'English only' variety, bilingual dictionaries *can* help learners to find out how to say 'x' or 'y' in English, i.e. you *can* look up what you don't know.

We should also note that a translation is often the clearest way of helping a learner understand what a word means. Look at the ways in which a learner's dictionary in English and a bilingual dictionary deal with the word *mustard*. (Examples 5 and 6.)

The *OALD* explanation is as clear as possible, but it still uses words which in themselves are difficult to understand. For a learner restricted by lack of vocabulary and unfamiliarity with English-speaking cultures, translation is the simplest solution.

OALD *Bilingual*
Example 5 *Example 6*

| **mus·tard** /'mʌstəd/ *n* **1** [U] plant with yellow flowers and (black or white) sharp-tasting seeds in long thin pods. **2 (a)** [U] (also **'mustard powder**) these seeds ground into powder. **(b)** [U. C] these seeds or this powder mixed into a strong-flavoured sauce with (esp) vinegar and served with savoury food: [attrib] *a mustard pot/jar/spoon*. **3** [U] darkish yellow colour (like the sauce made from the seeds of the mustard plant):[attrib] *a mustard (yellow) sweater*. **4** (idm) **keen as mustard** ⇨ KEEN¹. | **mustard** ['mʌstəd] *s.* **1** (*Gastr*) mostarda *f.* senape *f.* **2** (*Bot*) brassica *f.* **3** (*Bot*) (*black mustard*) senape *f* nera. **4** (*colour*) color *m* senape. senape *m.* ▭ (*fam*) *as keen as* ~ pieno di entusiasmo. |

So, both learner's dictionaries in English and bilingual dictionaries can be very useful in different ways. But where possible, bilingual dictionaries should be both modern and large – 'pocket' dictionaries can be extremely dangerous as they can encourage learners to believe that there are always convenient, 'exact' equivalents between words and do not provide explanations if different meanings are offered. In general we can say that the higher the level of the students, the more useful learner's dictionaries in English will be.

> ACTIVITY
>
> A Look again at the list of dictionaries which you made for the activity on page 92. Divide them into the two categories of:
>
> - Learner's dictionaries in English.
> - Bilingual dictionaries.
>
> Are any of the dictionaries on your list different from these two categories? If so, in what ways? Are there, for example, any dictionaries written for native speakers?
>
> B If possible, look also at the dictionary sections of some publishers' catalogues and decide which dictionaries your school most needs but doesn't have at present.

Note: Three useful titles for teachers are: *Working with Words* by Ruth Gairns and Stuart Redman (Cambridge 1986), *Using a Learner's Dictionary in the Classroom* by Shirley Burridge and Max Adam (Oxford free teacher's guide), *Dictionaries, Lexicography and Language Learning* edited by Robert Ilson (ELT Documents 120 – The British Council).

Questions and further activities

1 If you have access to some or all of the different types of dictionaries discussed in this chapter, look at the ways in which they deal with each of the words in the list below. Which dictionary do you find most useful for each of the words? Can you see any further advantages or disadvantages in any of these types of dictionaries?

for	furniture	neck
above	to look forward to	bank
which	to suggest	ice cream

2 Do you have a class set of dictionaries available? If so, do you think the dictionary chosen is the best one for your students and if it isn't, is it possible to change it? If you haven't got a class set, is it possible to get one?

3 If you have access to either Adrian Underhill's user guide (for the *OALD*) or Janet McAlpine's guide (for the *LDOCE*), work through it and try to find ten or more useful new ways in which your students can use a dictionary.

References

1 *Working with Words* by Ruth Gairns and Stuart Redman (Cambridge 1986)
2 *Using a Learner's Dictionary in the Classroom* by Shirley Burridge and Max Adam (Oxford)
3 *Dictionaries, Lexicography and Language Learning* edited by Roger Ilson (ELT Documents 120 – The British Council)
4 *Example 1* from *Longman Dictionary Skills Handbook* by Janet McAlpine (Longman 1988)
5 *Example 2* from *Longman Dictionary Of Contemporary English* (Longman 1992)
6 *Example 3* from *Collins Spanish Dictionary* (Collins 1988)
7 *Example 4* from *Collins Spanish Dictionary* (Collins 1988)
8 *Example 5* from *Oxford Advanced Learner's Dictionary* (Oxford 1990)
9 *Example 6* from *Collins Sansoni Italian Dictionary* (Collins 1988)

9 Basic classroom English

The purpose of this final chapter is to summarise the *absolutely basic* classroom English that all teachers and students should know and use. In order to do this, I've focused on four main areas for teachers and four approximately equivalent areas for students:

Teachers	Students
1 Getting students to do things.	*Responding to the teacher's instructions.*
2 Getting information from the students.	*Giving the teacher information.*
3 Giving students information and permission.	*Asking the teacher for information and permission.*
4 General interaction with the students.	*General interaction with the teacher.*

There's a table for each area (see pages 99 – 102) and within each area there are different 'sub-areas'. For example, *Getting students to do things* includes giving instructions, organising activities, and so on. It's important to emphasise that the language in the four tables really is the *minimum*. *All* of this language is vital if English is to be the main language in the classroom. Now, read through the four tables and ask yourself the following questions:

- Do you know all the expressions for teachers?
- Do you *use* all of them?
- How many of the students' expressions do your groups know?
- Do you insist on them using all the expressions which they do know, or do you sometimes allow 'lazy' L1 use?

TABLE 1

Getting students to do things		Responding to the teacher's instructions
Instructions Organising activities	Open your book at page 10. Look at the picture. Get into pairs. You've got 5 mins. I'll give you Okay. That's enough. Have you finished? Everybody should finish by 10.15 am. You hand in the homework on Friday.	
Requesting	Could you stop now? Would everybody be finishing off now? Will get your books out? their stop talking, please.	*Okay, Fritz.* *Yes, Miss Lee.* *Right, Maria.* *Mr Erikson.*
Suggesting and advising	Let's do that again? Why don't you use the present perfect? What about a game? a different activity? starting again? doing a dictation?	*Yes, okay.* *do some listening.* *I'd prefer to finish this exercise.* *play a game* *I don't mind!*
Eliciting correction	Is that right? Do you think that's correct? No, that's not quite right. Can anyone help? Anyone else? Pronunciation!	
Discipline in the classroom	Could you see me after the lesson, please? Settle down, please. Stop messing about. speaking in French, etc. Okay, that's enough, stop talking and get on with your work. Be quiet!	

TABLE 2

Getting information from the students		*Giving the teacher information*
Eliciting	What's this?	It's a dog. horse. an umbrella.
	What are they doing?	They're having lunch. waiting for a bus.
	How do you say *albero* in English?	It's a tree.
Taking the register	Is anyone absent?	Yes, X is. X and Y are.
	Does anyone know where X is?	Yes, he's seeing Z. she's taking an exam.
	Were you absent last Tuesday? yesterday? last week?	Yes, I my son was ill. my mother
Checking answers	Can you answer number X?	Yes, it's ..... No, I'm sorry I don't know. I can't remember.
	Did anyone have anything else?	Yes, I wrote ..... put ..... had .....
	Do you agree?	Yes, I do. No, I don't. I think it's .....
Finding out about difficulties and problems	What's the problem? matter?	I can't see the board. do the exercise. I don't understand. I don't agree. I haven't brought my pen.
	Why are you late?	I'm sorry, I missed the bus. I got caught in a traffic jam.
	Have you done the homework?	No, I'm sorry, I didn't have time.
	Where's your book?	I'm sorry, I've forgotten it.

TABLE 3

Asking the teacher for information and permission		Giving students information and permission
Asking about the lesson	What do we have to do? Which page are we on? When's the homework for? I've finished, what should I do now?	Turn to page 10 please. We're on page 70. Homework is for Friday. Can you carry on with the next exercise, please? Yesterday, we did a role play. Now, we're going to do some reading. That's all for today. See you next Thursday. You can go now.
Asking about language	How do you say X in English?	If we want to say X in English talk about future arrangements we use the preposition *above*. the present continuous.
	What does Y mean? What's the difference between X and Y? How do you spell X? How do you pronounce this word? Is this correct? Why is it wrong?	Y means 'albero'.
Asking for repetition	Sorry? Could you repeat that? Could you explain that again?	

Requests	Could I leave early?
	   have a piece of paper?
	   have more time?
	Could you write that?
	   turn the volume up?
	   speak more slowly?
		Yes, of course./I'd rather you didn't.
		Yes, here you are./No, I'm sorry, I haven't got any.
		
		Yes, certainly.

TABLE 4

General interaction with the students		General interaction with the teacher
Greetings	Good morning. afternoon. evening. Have a nice weekend. evening. See you tomorrow. on Monday. next week.	*The same as the 'teacher' language.*
Offering help	Are you okay? there any problems? Do you understand what to do? You don't look very sure. Shall I give you a hand? (Shall I help you?) Does anybody need any help?	*Everything's okay, thanks.* *Yes. / No, not really.* *I'm having a bit of difficulty with number 6.* *Yes, I do.*
Offering encouragement	Come on. You can do it. It's not as difficult as it looks. Just do your best. (Do as well as you can.)	*Okay, I'll try.* *. . . . , but it really is too difficult.*
Praising	Good. Well done. You've worked really hard. Excellent.	*Thanks / Thank you very much.*
Apologising	Sorry. I'm sorry about that.	*That's alright.* *okay.* *Never mind, it doesn't matter.*
Thanking	I'm very grateful, I really appreciate it, thanks. Thanks very much.	*You're welcome.* *Don't mention it.* *That's okay.*

Note: The language in these tables is based on Standard British English. It will need to be adapted in situations where the students' goal is to learn a different variety, such as Standard American English, West African or Indian English.

Using the tables

General

- Sometimes what the teacher says doesn't need the students to say anything in response. For example, in *Giving instructions* the group will often just carry out the instruction.
- In some cases it's impossible to say what the student's response is likely to be. For instance, the response to *Eliciting correction* will obviously depend on what's being corrected.
- Two 'items' of language are missing from the tables, because otherwise they would have to go almost everywhere; they are *excuse me*, and students' names. Students need to learn *excuse me* in order to begin any interaction with the teacher, e.g. *Excuse me, I don't understand*. When talking to individual students, the teacher should try to use their names as much as possible, for the reasons discussed in chapter 6. *Please* should obviously follow many instructions, requests, phrases for asking about things, and so on. At higher levels more complex language should be used by both teachers and students.

Teachers' language

With lower level groups, many different techniques can be used to reinforce the meaning of what the teacher is saying. For example:

- Gesture – point to your ear or to the cassette recorder when saying *We're going to do some listening*. Use a culturally appropriate gesture for silence before or after saying *Be quiet!*
- Mime – mime opening a book for *Open your books at page . . . .* Mime walking, jogging, swimming, etc. as you teach the appropriate verbs.

In many cases it's better to use English supported by one of these techniques than to go into the L1 (see the discussion of the L1 in chapters 1 – 4).

Students' language

Students need to be *taught* the expressions. It's a good idea to keep a check-list of 'student expressions' for each class and tick each one off once you've taught it to the class.

> ACTIVITY
>
> Write a check-list of 'student expressions' for one of your own classes. Fix a date by which you want the students to know the expressions on it and tick each one off as they learn it.

What if they don't know the structures?

There's no reason why the students should have studied the *structures* used in the expressions before they learn the expressions themselves. For example, students don't need to have studied the present simple in order to learn *I don't understand* (they should learn this phrase in their first lesson!), etc. This is for two reasons. It means that students can learn vital phrases as early as necessary and it gives them a sort of 'pre-introduction' to the structures, which can be a big help when they come to study them.

Questions and further activities

1 Can you think of any other expressions which you feel are essential for students and/or teachers to know? If so, do they fit into the categories which I've used, or are other categories necessary?
2 What's your reaction if, for instance, you accidentally stand on a student's foot or knock a book off his or her desk? Do you instinctively apologise in English or in the L1? What does this indicate as regards your feelings about the roles of the two languages?

Appendix: 10 tips for teachers who don't know their students' language

A significant number of teachers of monolingual classes don't have a common language with their students other than English. Most, but not all, of these teachers are native speakers of English. The following suggestions are specifically for such teachers.

1 Learn the students' language: go to classes, set up a conversation exchange, study on your own, etc. Or, at the very least, learn *about* the language and the students' likely linguistic problems. For example, through books such as:
   - *Learner English* by Michael Swan and Bernard Smith (Cambridge 1987)
   - *The Longman English – Chinese Dictionary of Common Errors* by J.B. Heaton and N.D. Turton (Longman 1990)
   - *Common Errors in English* (for speakers of African languages) by David Jowitt and Silas Nnamonu (Longman 1985)
   - *En inglés? Sin Problemas – Common Problems in English for Spanish Speakers* by Mike O'Neill (Nelson 1989)
   - *Sta anglika; kanena provlima – Common Problems in English for Greek Speakers* by Hara Garoufalia Middle (Nelson forthcoming).

2 Where possible, avoid getting stuck in native speaker 'cliques' and 'ghettoes'. Try to become involved in local events and to meet local people outside the classroom.

3 Respect your students' views on classrooms, teachers and learning; use learner training techniques with sensitivity and tact.

4 Make sure that you know what is considered 'normal' student behaviour in class; it may be very different from in your own culture. This is especially important as regards discipline and control with young learners.

5 Liaise and co-operate as much as possible with non-native speaker colleagues (particularly concerning points 3 and 4).

6 *Don't* impose your own culture on the learners. The fact that they're learning English doesn't necessarily mean that they need or want to know a great deal about British, American, Australian etc. culture.

7 Don't pretend that the L1 doesn't exist. Many learners are proud of their L1 and want the teacher to be aware of this: this is particularly true in the case of 'minority' languages.

8 Allow occasional L1 use, for example 'L1 rest periods', learners helping each other with difficulties, etc.

9 If you're studying the L1, don't use it in the classroom unless your level is very substantially higher than your students' level in English. Stick to direct method!

10 In general, be a learner as well as a teacher – this is more rewarding and helps to gain the students' respect.